LONG HAUL

ALSO BY FRANK FIGLIUZZI

The FBI Way: Inside the Bureau's Code of Excellence

LONG HAUL

*HUNTING
THE
HIGHWAY
SERIAL KILLERS*

FRANK FIGLIUZZI

MARINER BOOKS

New York   Boston

HarperCollins books may be purchased for educational, business, or sales promotional use. For information, please email the Special Markets Department at SPsales@harpercollins.com.

The Mariner flag design is a registered trademark of HarperCollins Publishers LLC.

A hardcover edition of this book was published in 2024 by Mariner Books.

FIRST MARINER BOOKS PAPERBACK EDITION PUBLISHED 2025.

Designed by Renata DiBiase

Library of Congress Cataloging-in-Publication Data has been applied for.

ISBN 978-0-06-326516-5

25 26 27 28 29 LBC 5 4 3 2 1

Dedicated to the survivors and thrivers of the scourge of human trafficking, the passionate professionals who work with victims to make miracles out of misery, and the law enforcers who stop killers from killing again. This story is also for the stalwart American truckers who feed their own families by getting food to our tables and who likely put this book in your hand.

CONTENTS

AUTHOR'S NOTE   xi

INTRODUCTION   1

CHAPTER 1: **SUNDAY WITH MIKE**   9

CHAPTER 2: **THE FBI CRIME ANALYST**   18

CHAPTER 3: **GIRLS NEXT DOOR**   30

CHAPTER 4: **THE PIONEER PROFESSOR**   45

CHAPTER 5: **OLD-TIMER**   62

CHAPTER 6: **MONDAY WITH MIKE**   72

CHAPTER 7: **THE OKLAHOMA CRIME ANALYST**   100

CHAPTER 8: **CROSSING THE RUBICON**   107

CHAPTER 9: **THE PIONEER PROFESSOR**   117

CHAPTER 10: **TUESDAY WITH MIKE**   121

CHAPTER 11: **THE OKLAHOMA CRIME ANALYST**   135

CHAPTER 12: **PROGRAMMED CODE**   144

CHAPTER 13: **A STARFISH IN THE DESERT**   148

CHAPTER 14: **WEDNESDAY WITH MIKE**   164

CHAPTER 15: **THE OKLAHOMA CRIME ANALYST**   174

CHAPTER 16: **THURSDAY WITH MIKE**   179

CHAPTER 17: **THE FBI CRIME ANALYST**   198

CHAPTER 18: **FRIDAY WITH MIKE**   207

CHAPTER 19: **SATURDAY WITH MIKE**   220

CHAPTER 20: **SURVIVOR TO THRIVER**   227

EPILOGUE   233

ACKNOWLEDGMENTS   247

NOTES   251

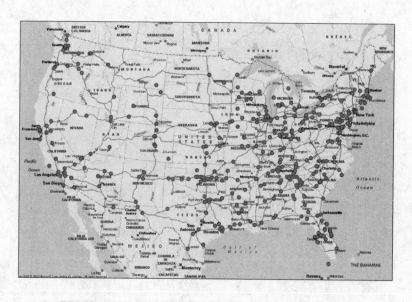

An FBI Highway Serial Killings Initiative map plotting more than 500 cases from its database. The dots mark where bodies or remains have been found along American highways.

Courtesy of the FBI

AUTHOR'S NOTE

To protect privacy and security, some of the names and places in this true-crime book are pseudonyms. For example, Hannah, Mike, and Dale are aliases, as are the names of their family members, associates, and some employers. The FBI crime analyst requested an alias. Individuals who could not be contacted for their consent or who are described as engaging in potentially criminal conduct were also provided pseudonyms. Hannah, Mike, and Dale signed legal releases to allow their stories to be told. I'm grateful.

LONG HAUL

INTRODUCTION

It was early morning on April Fools' Day in 1990 when Arizona state trooper Mike Miller spotted a truck with its hazard lights blinking on the shoulder of I-10 in Casa Grande. Miller donned his trooper hat, stepped out of his patrol car, strode up to the big rig, and looked inside. That's when the lawman saw her: a young woman shackled in a makeshift torture chamber in the rear of the cab. As soon as she saw him, she began screaming for help. The fuzzy lion slippers on her feet only magnified the fact that she was otherwise totally naked.

The driver was the quintessential killer trucker. The cops, prosecutors, and media bestowed the well-deserved moniker "Truck Stop Killer" on Robert Ben Rhoades; it was a name earned in evil. He was the one all other trucker killers would be measured against—for his volume of victims, the span of his murderous spree, and the sheer terror inflicted on his prey. He worked as a long-haul trucker for almost twenty years, and for at least fifteen of those years, Rhoades kidnapped, tortured, raped, and killed—leaving as many as fifty suspected victims in his wake. Rhoades built a traveling torture chamber in the rear of his semi, and hunted the highways for his next kill.

Rhoades was busted for kidnapping the screaming woman the trooper found, but it was the discovery of his final murder victim—Regina Walters—that put Rhoades away for life.

Regina was only fourteen years old when she and her boyfriend, Ricky, slipped out of their troubled family lives in Pasadena, Texas, to hitchhike their way to a fantasy future. But the only thing in their future was darkness. In February 1990, near Houston, Rhoades offered the two teens a ride. Ricky didn't last long. He was a mere speed bump, slowing Rhoades down briefly but not stopping him from kidnapping Regina and raping her at times and places of his choosing. She endured endless weeks of barbaric pain; her flesh was torn by fishhooks and she was handcuffed to the ceiling of the tomb-like dungeon inside Rhoades's rig.

The demons consuming Rhoades's soul weren't sated by the mental and physical torture of Regina. They demanded more. So Rhoades extended his cruelty by calling Regina's father one month after she vanished. Without giving his name, Rhoades informed the anguished man, "I made some changes. I cut her hair."

Indeed, the last photos ever taken of Regina confirmed her brunette hair had been roughly cut into a boyish bob. Yet for those who view those final, ghastly images of Regina, it's not her hair that's forever seared into their consciousness; it's the horror on her face. Those haunting displays depict Regina in the final minutes before she was strangled to death, her body left to decompose in an abandoned farmhouse in Illinois. In the photos, Regina, forced into a black dress and high heels, stands in front of the camera, her face contorted, her eyes revealing abject fear. The teen girl's arms are extended forward and her palms are raised as if she's imploring Rhoades's demons not to return. But return they did.

FBI agent Mark Young said Regina's forensic report revealed "something invaluable." He explained, "Her pubic hair had been shaved prior to death. This was the signature aspect of the killer I would be looking for."

If only Rhoades were the last of the killer truckers for him to find. That would mean no more victims would suffer brutal deaths at the hands of highway barbarians. No more Rhoadeses, no more Reginas. There would be no need for the FBI and the police to look for serial killers' signatures. But that would be a fool's fantasy.

In my first book, *The FBI Way: Inside the Bureau's Code of Excellence,* I shared with readers what I already knew—lessons I'd learned in over two decades as an FBI special agent. I wanted to convey how people might apply the FBI's values-based performance methods to their own quest for excellence. I wrote about what I knew so that others might understand it.

This book is different.

Long Haul began in 2021 when an FBI criminal analyst told me about the Bureau's Highway Serial Killings (HSK) Initiative. The analyst (whose real name I will not use to protect her identity) explained that over the years, multiple truckers had been convicted of serial murders, and today the FBI believes there are hundreds—yes, hundreds—of unsolved killings that were also likely committed by truckers. The FBI analyst told me that the Bureau had compiled a list of an astonishing 850 murders believed to be linked to long-haul truckers. I was floored by these revelations.

I decided I had to know more, dig deeper, comprehend what

was happening. As Stephen Covey wrote in *The Seven Habits of Highly Effective People*, "Seek first to understand, then to be understood." Writing about what I had lived was easy. Writing about other people's reality—the reality around the HSK—would be harder. I needed to experience the components and cultures in the HSK myself. I spent months considering how to accomplish this and a year of my life learning and then writing about what I had found.

I'm trained to discern what isn't necessarily apparent to others. The pedophile on the edge of the playground. The chalk mark that signals a spy's dead-drop site. The surveillance team that tracked me on a business trip to China. To see those things, you must first learn everything you can about what you are trying to find, who you are looking for, and where to look. For this book, I needed to see the good and the bad to have any hope of understanding the ugly. What I discovered were entire subcultures that most Americans know little about.

I understand more now. I understand enough to share what I came to grasp: Hundreds of murders have been committed along our nation's highways. Many of those homicides are connected, but many are not. Those murders were committed by multiple—yes, multiple—serial killers. Some of those homicides have been solved, some of the killers apprehended, but many—far too many—have not.

According to the FBI, in most cases of highway homicide, long-haul truckers are responsible.

Long-haul truckers exist for days or weeks at a time in a world of their own. They speak their own language, eat at their own establishments, sleep in their own rigs. Part cowboy, part fighter pilot, part hermit, long-haul truckers glide along the edge of a certain seam in the fabric of our society—the seam that separates their reality from ours.

Killer truckers exploit that seam—that little-known long-haul subculture, the one where we share the same roads but different realities.

There is a second seam to this book, the one that separates the truckers' victims from the justice they deserve. That line divides the drug-addicted truck-stop female sex workers from their estranged families, many of whom don't know—or don't care to know—the women's whereabouts. It is the nature of those victims and their victimology that keeps overworked, underpaid cops from prioritizing those cases. It's who those victims are and what they have been made to do to eke out an existence that keeps communities from becoming outraged and demanding answers to the murders in their midst.

These victims—many of them, at least—live in their own roadside subculture, seen but unseen, known but unknown. Same world, different reality.

Seam three is where cops and crime analysts do their thing, mostly apart from the people they protect, the people they investigate, and, often, one another. This is the seam that separates one police jurisdiction from the one a mile away, five hundred miles away, two thousand miles away. It is the border between the state where a killer finds his female victims, the state where he murders those women, and the state where the bodies are dumped. It's in that seam where city cops, state investigators, county deputies, and FBI crime analysts—all in different places—try to connect dots they don't know exist among murders they've never heard of in locations they've never looked.

Those puzzle solvers also have their own subculture, their own language, their own way of moving through their world. A world inhabited by them, the truckers, and the trafficked.

For this book, I pulled on the threads of those three seams to try to unravel the mystery of multiple murders. Along the way I discovered something as intriguing as the murders themselves— maybe even more so. There are three fascinating, largely obscure subcultures, separate yet braided together, that sometimes collide atop cold autopsy tables at county coroner's offices. Those subcultures—of truckers, trafficked victims, and investigators— and their stories make this book less of a whodunnit and more of a "Who are they?"

Who are they, those largely unknown entities who exist beyond the bubbles in which most of us spend our isolated, oblivious lives?

Who are the truckers who transport the food we eat, the furniture we sit on, the clothing we wear? What makes them choose to ride the roads solo for weeks or months on end? When do they see their kids, their spouses—if they even have any? How much do they earn? Are serial killers drawn to this job, or does the job cultivate the killer? Or is it both?

And who are the trafficked victims we choose not to see, the ones on the other side of the interstate rest stop—the truck side? The women who advertise on the internet that they are "trucker-friendly"? The ones with the long-sleeved shirts that hide their track marks who are trying to earn some cash so they can make more track marks? How does this become their reality? Whose daughters are they? Whose mothers are they? When they go missing, does anyone know? Does anyone care? Who are the people who control them?

Which law enforcement minds, which crime analysts in which jurisdictions, figure this all out? Who realizes that some of these murders are connected? What is the FBI doing about it? Can they stop it from continuing?

In pursuit of answers to these mysteries, I submerged myself in others' sometimes dark, sometimes desperate, sometimes murderous realities. I heard it from them and saw it for myself. It became my own personal long haul.

CHAPTER 1

SUNDAY WITH MIKE

She asked me not to use her name. It's the nature of her work; sometimes serial killers can be unpleasant.

Catherine DeVane (an alias) leads the FBI's Highway Serial Killings Initiative. I asked her, while we recorded our conversation, whether the FBI was really blaming all this killing on long-haul truckers.

"Unfortunately, the commonalities we're looking at with this particular initiative—the HSK—are dealing with the long-haul trucking industry. I mean, we're not saying that every long-haul trucker out there is a serial offender or even involved in criminal activity. I mean, I had family members who were involved in truck driving, but they weren't involved in killing people or raping people."

She added that there were thousands of cases in the Violent Criminal Apprehension Program—ViCAP—crime database that weren't connected to the highways. But with the HSK, she said, "The folks that we're looking at, unfortunately, are involved in the long-haul trucking industry. What we have found is because they travel the highways, they don't have that employer sitting there, so they've got some anonymity as to what they are doing, how long it takes them to get from point A to point B. But that's why this initiative was designed. Let's see who's traveling those highways."

That was good enough for me. If I was going to understand the cultures beneath the HSK, I needed to start by learning about long-haul trucking from those who did it for a living. I had to travel those highways and walk in their shoes.

What are you wearing?

Mike texted me from his late-arriving Spirit Airlines flight from Fort Lauderdale to Chicago. I was camped out in the gate area fighting sleep hours after my own flight's arrival—just me and the low hum of the overnight cleaning crew vacuuming acres of carpet.

Dude, I'm the only one at the gate. It's 1:30 a.m., I texted back.

Gotcha. You can't miss me. Short stocky guy, big beard, gray shirt, black basketball shorts, Mike replied.

He was right. I didn't miss him. Mike was a twenty-eight-year-old fireplug with feet. He was five six and weighed about 270 pounds. We shook hands, and Mike—annoyed by his late arrival—muttered that this flight was always late. We talked as we walked. I asked him why he kept choosing this night flight on a chronically late, low-budget airline.

"I have integrity—I'm not going to milk the boss for an expensive airfare or a hotel."

Mike lived in south Florida. The trucking company Mike drove for was based outside of Chicago. As we lugged our duffel bags through the terminal in search of the rideshare pickup area, Mike cautioned me that it was way too late and he was much too sleepy to start any heavy discussions. I agreed; my brain wasn't likely to absorb much at this hour anyway. The lot where Mike's truck waited was about forty minutes out of the city; when we got there, we'd grab maybe a couple of hours of shut-eye in his truck's sleeper berth, then hit the road just after dawn.

From a couple of prior phone calls with Mike, I sensed he was a talker. In fact, that's why I was grateful when he'd agreed to tolerate my presence in his truck for a week. If I was going to learn something about modern long-haul trucking, I needed a crash course taught by a willing teacher. And Mike—despite warning that he was in no mood to talk—started talking. This fireplug might be a fire hose.

As we sat in the back of our Uber, Mike seemed to finally start processing the logistics of me being his guest for the week. "I think there's an extra pillow in the bunk. Did you bring a pillow? I know there's a blanket. Pretty sure about the blanket."

No, I hadn't brought a pillow—or a blanket.

Between the airport terminal and the truck lot, Mike started to download his story to me. "I was a fifteen-year-old busboy in an Italian restaurant who saw what the chefs were doing and wanted to do that. I begged the manager to give me any job in the kitchen—prep work, whatever." His uncle—a player in commercial real estate and restaurant properties—picked up the pricey tuition tab at the Culinary Institute of America (CIA) in Hyde Park, New York.

Mike thrived at CIA. He was a driven type A leader, a self-described "Let's get it done" guy. In the fast-paced in-kitchen assignments, when his fellow students' indecision and inexperience devolved into culinary chaos, Mike took over. "I need two on dish," he'd call out. "Let's sweep this floor."

In the breakneck pace of the flagship school's kitchens, a struggling student was a weight around the neck of his unfortunate partner. Mike was often partnered with another top student in the class. The pair ran circles around everyone in the kitchen assignments. Other students started complaining that it wasn't fair when they were partnered with one particularly challenged student because their grades suffered. Eventually, Mike said to the instructors, "Give me that guy. Give me the guy who's struggling." Well, that student, then partnered with Mike, ended up graduating with high grades.

That's the kind of guy Mike is. That's the impact he has on those around him.

Mike did well, especially in the kitchen, and got nice job offers after graduation. Then one day, back home in Florida, "I woke up to find my father cold, dead." Mike's dad's death was unexpected, and Mike and his brother had to settle their dad's affairs. His dad had been into motorcycles and cars; if it went fast, Mike's dad wanted it, wanted to drive it. That became part of Mike's DNA. Today, whenever Mike was home, he worked on his own pet project, a 2001 Lexus GS 300. This was Mike's baby. Later, he showed me the baby's photos. He was putting a turbo engine in it, all the bells and whistles. A "Japanese rice burner," he called it. Mike wasn't particularly concerned with political correctness.

Mike poured himself into being a chef. "I'm a fisherman, I'd fish every day as a kid, so my favorite cooking was ocean-to-table, any fish dish."

There was a job at Racks Fish House and Oyster Bar in Delray Beach. Then a couple more restaurant roles, including Sun,

Surf, Sand, an upscale place in Fort Lauderdale. But Mike began to suffer, badly, from gout, which he was genetically pre-disposed to. It was painful; he couldn't walk, couldn't be on his feet. He started to call in sick even on busy Friday nights, not something that went over well in the restaurant business. Mike knew his health was becoming a burden not only to him but to his bosses and his coworkers. The money a new chef earned wasn't that great to begin with, and now that money was drying up. Mike had bills to pay. He was broke. He needed cash, and he needed to be off his feet.

"But why trucking?" I asked.

Mike told me he wasn't an office guy; he had never been that guy in the cubicle. "I'm a car enthusiast, gearhead; so was my father. We always had dirt bikes, go-karts; we considered these our toys. I always thought trucks were cool."

Mike started researching online to learn what he had to do to get a CDL, a commercial driver's license. "I had no money, I sold my motorcycle to get my CDL. My mom spotted me seven hundred dollars the first time I even went out on the road. I chose a training school that was ten minutes from my house. They didn't even teach me how to disconnect a trailer. My school let you take the test when you felt you were ready as long as you met a minimum of three days on each of the required exercises—backing up, offset or parallel parking, alley dock. There were three written tests at the DMV, then a DOT physical, then a trip back to DMV to get my license. Start to finish, it was about three weeks," Mike told me.

That's not much, I thought, *for being allowed to pilot tons of steel on wheels across our nation's highways.*

Then the job search began. One day, Mike was on his laptop and found a site for new CDL drivers looking for work. Yet what he mostly saw there were guys complaining that a newbie driver had to start out at one of the major companies, and those places could be brutal to work for and not great in the pay department. *This is shitty,* Mike thought. But one guy on the site posted that he worked for a small company out of Chicago called Ox and Eagle. That piqued Mike's interest. He messaged the guy and got a response.

"How much do you want to make? What do you make now?" the man asked Mike. It turned out this guy was the lead dispatcher for Ox and Eagle. Pretty quickly, Mike was introduced to Andrei, Ox and Eagle's owner. After a long phone conversation, Andrei told Mike, "I'll pay for your flight to Chicago."

His friends thought he was crazy.

"What is this company?" Mike's friends asked him. "Are you leaving Florida for Chicago in the middle of winter?" Mike's mom even had a private investigator check it out.

Andrei was supposed to pick Mike up at the airport, but he got stuck in a business meeting. No big deal for Andrei, who told Mike he'd pay for the Uber ride to a drug-testing place to start the hiring process. When Mike arrived at the testing site, they asked him for four hundred dollars. Andrei paid this fee over the phone, and Mike was impressed. "I felt better," Mike said.

Finally, Mike met Andrei at his office. He offered Mike coffee, among other things. "Are you hungry? Here's the keys to my Mercedes—go explore Chicago, get something to eat while you wait for your driver trainer to arrive." Now Mike was really impressed. He called his friends to tell them he was holding the keys to the boss's Mercedes.

Mike's trainer—the presumably seasoned driver selected to impart all things trucking—was twenty-one-year-old Noah. Noah had worked for Melton, a flatbed company with a specialized three-week course in their parking lot that truckers call the Harvard of flatbedding. Noah met some guys at this Melton school, made friends, got their numbers. "Then Noah meets this trucker that tells him to stop working at Melton," Mike said, "that he can make double at Ox and Eagle. So now Noah has a bunch of these guys in a group chat that he recruited to work here—we talk to these guys all day on the phone while driving. In fact, we all decided to meet in Austin where one of us lives. We had a great time. Great town."

Mike knew why I was riding with him. I told him my interest in killer truckers had become a quest to learn more about culture, including Mike's. I wanted to know what truckers did, how they worked, why they chose trucking in the first place. Mike was a young, relatively new trucker, so he was still trying to wrap his head around the culture. Mike shared an initial observation with me.

"A lot of truckers don't have a place to live, no place to go; they live in the truck. It could explain why so many truckers can be rude to each other, heckling over the CB or at truck stops over parking spots. I have hobbies. I bought another motorcycle. I have a mother, my mother's fiancé, my brother, my friends. Other guys, other truckers—they may have nothing."

What Mike tried to tell me was that he had a life, a life with other people in it. A life outside his truck. Duly noted.

Noah decided to train Mike, the kid from Florida, in white-out blizzard conditions in the Rocky Mountains of Montana and Wyoming. It was cruel and unusual punishment for Mike, who would never forget the heart-pounding, sweat-soaked days of simply trying not to die or kill anyone else. At the time, Mike didn't know the difference between a flatbed on a truck and a flat note on a keyboard. His on-the-job training took place over the course of just six weeks. Then Mike was ready to drive on his own.

That was it. Trained. Mike joined the ranks of the one million semitruck drivers in the United States.

For the next seven weeks, Mike drove a truck belonging to some guy named Sergey. That too was a flatbed. Now it was my turn to be educated on what it took to drive, load, and off-load that kind of big rig.

For Mike, CDL school was just something he had to get through so he could start working and begin to really learn the job. He gave me a taste of his brake knowledge gleaned during his sojourn in the Rockies. "There's an engine brake, called a Jake brake, and there's a trailer brake. In the winter, if your trailer starts coming out from under you, a fishtail, most drivers will just slam on their Jake brakes, but what they should do is apply the trailer brake and then hit the gas—speed up—and then the trailer will straighten out."

I hoped we wouldn't need to do that.

"Then Andrei tells me he bought me a brand-new truck. He gives me an address in Kentucky to go pick up a new trailer for the truck." Along with his new ride, Mike was given a new electronic tablet logbook and new straps and chains to secure his loads. "I drove that truck for eighty thousand miles last year. Then I traded trucks to add a bunk bed to the sleeper berth so I could start training new drivers. My buddy tells me he's getting his CDL, so I trained him and kept this truck."

Just like that, the student became the teacher. And Mike would provide my education during our week together on the road.

At this point, the Uber pulled into a large lot filled with big rigs in an industrial part of town. Mike directed the driver toward his assigned truck. It was dark except for an occasional overhead light, so all the chrome truck grilles that grimaced back at us looked alike to me. Mike spotted the truck number on the side of his rig. Bingo.

It was about three a.m., and Sunday had crept into Monday. Mike did a walk-around safety check before we entered the truck, and I tossed my bags up onto the top bunk in the sleeper berth. The time for talking was over. The time for sleeping was a few hours ago.

As Mike instructed, I pulled my bags back down from the top bunk and dropped them on the passenger seat—a drill I'd reverse in the morning and repeat twice each day. Then I removed my boots and slipped through a mesh magnetic closure curtain into the cramped, dark berth. I grabbed a handle on the bunk, planted one foot high on a small countertop, and hoisted myself up into the top bunk. Mercifully, there was a pillow—lumpy, with no pillowcase, but a pillow. There was also a towel-size paper-thin blue blanket that I attempted to draw up and around at least part of me against the Chicago night chill in the truck.

The alarm was set for six a.m.

CHAPTER 2

THE FBI CRIME ANALYST

"Dump sites, weapons used, bindings used, the place or position in which the victim's body was found—was the body in water? A culvert? Was the body mutilated or sexually abused?" Catherine DeVane recited the commonalities assessed by crime analysts across a spectrum of murders. Commonalities that connect the dots that form a line that points to a serial killer.

Catherine rattled off the kinds of things that constitute commonalities in terms of the offenders. That's where the bindings, the weapons, the dump sites, the proximity to water all come into play.

Catherine knows. She's led the FBI Highway Serial Killings Initiative for seventeen years. She's a crime analyst in Behavioral Analysis Unit (BAU) 4, based in the Critical Incident Response Group in Quantico, Virginia. The HSK team, with the help of data entered by police departments around the nation, helps agencies match the commonalities across the crime scenes and the victims and hopefully match the crime to a killer. There are 850 cases in the HSK Initiative. That's the number of murders that the FBI believes long-haul truckers have committed.

Catherine grew up in a small town in east Texas. She never envisioned doing what she does or seeing what she sees—"the worst of the worst," as she calls it. Catherine can eat a salad at her desk while poring over crime scene images of grisly slaughter. She's learned to "compartmentalize" what she sees on her computer screen, but it's not easy.

For example, how do you compartmentalize the evil that took place in Bruce Mendenhall's killing chamber?

Nashville Metro PD homicide detective Pat Postiglione caught up with long-hauler Bruce Mendenhall sitting in his vehicle at a Nashville, Tennessee, truck stop.

The veteran detective asked Mendenhall, "Are you the person we've been looking for?"

Mendenhall looked at the detective, shrugged, and responded, "If you say so."

Illinois-based Bruce D. Mendenhall was arrested at the same truck stop where he murdered twenty-five-year-old Sarah Nicole Hulbert in 2007. In court, prosecutors described the cab of his truck as a "killing chamber"; from it, investigators recovered "a rifle, a nightstick, tape, handcuffs, latex gloves, sex toys, and a bag of bloody clothing" with traces of the DNA of five different women. Mendenhall, who liked to shoot his victims in the head after he wrapped them in plastic and duct tape, received life sentences for murdering two women, one whose naked corpse was discovered tossed in a garbage can at the same Nashville stop where he was arrested. But he had more victims.

After he was busted, Bruce confessed to similar murders across different states. He told detectives he had murdered six women near truck stops in Tennessee, Indiana, Georgia, and Alabama. He was also connected to the killing of Carma Purpura, a thirty-one-year-old mother of two who had been missing since

2007 and was last seen at a Flying J truck stop in south Indianapolis, Indiana. Her remains weren't found and identified until August 2011. Carma couldn't point the police to Mendenhall, but her belongings could. Her bloody clothing, her ATM card, and her cell phone were in Bruce's truck. DNA testing confirmed the blood belonged to someone related to Carma's parents, which helped confirm the belongings were hers.

In 2010, Mendenhall was convicted of the first-degree murder of Hulbert and sentenced to life. While in prison, Mendenhall told two inmates he'd pay them to kill three witnesses who were going to testify against him. That scheme tacked thirty additional years to his sentence.

Mendenhall slaughtered Samantha Winters too. Her naked body was found in a trash can at a truck stop in Lebanon, Tennessee, on June 6, 2007. Like the others, Samantha had also died of gunshot wounds from Bruce's .22-caliber pistol. In 2018, Mendenhall was found guilty of Samantha's murder. He was convicted of first-degree murder and of the abuse of a corpse, which meant another life sentence for the murder and a two-year term for the abuse.

After a decade behind bars, Mendenhall was transferred from Tennessee to Indiana to finally stand trial for killing Carma, one more of at least nine of his alleged victims. His own DNA tied Bruce to Carma, as did the blood spatter and the knife inside his truck cab.

The police suspected Mendenhall in two or three other murders, but he couldn't have committed the hundreds of other unsolved cases in the HSK files, certainly not the ones in areas that Mendenhall was nowhere near at the time. His killing chamber held the answers to a lot of mysteries, but it couldn't solve them all.

The FBI publicly acknowledged the HSK in 2009. They had no choice—there were too many bodies across too many jurisdictions and not enough answers. There was a map of the murders linked to the initiative with red dots that signified bodies discovered along America's highways. While there were red dots everywhere on this map, if you stared at it long enough, you'd see it—a horizontal trail across the south-central United States. That line was Interstate 40. I-40 ran from Wilmington, North Carolina, to Barstow, California. And those red dots, like blood spatter, ran through places like Raleigh, Nashville, Memphis, Little Rock, Oklahoma City, Amarillo, Albuquerque, and Flagstaff.

BAU 4 is staffed by supervisory special agents, crime analysts, and major case specialists, but the team that connects the HSK dots from within a special database are entirely crime analysts—no badges, no guns. This work requires different tools: computer programs, brainpower, and experience. Over 850 of the multitude of violent crimes in the FBI's ViCAP database are murders that fit the HSK's criteria: female victims of opportunity, close to the highway, often near rest stops, and dumped close to the road.

Many of these cases are considered solved, but most of them—hundreds—are not.

Catherine shared with me the two types of offenders she sees in her cases. There are those who want to "control life and death," who want to "feel the power of controlling the outcome." These are killers who take their time, who mutilate and sexually abuse their victims before ending their lives.

Then there are the killers who, as Catherine said, "Don't want to have sex—they just want to kill someone." Those murderers kill faster.

And there is this: Many of these cases involve what Catherine calls "multiple serials." That means there are several killers who are each personally responsible for committing more than one of the murders.

Let me say that again: There is enough evidence of similarities among different clusters of killings for the FBI to say with confidence that there are multiple homicidal maniacs on our nation's highways.

I asked how many potential suspects HSK was looking at— how many truckers wanted to control life and death or just simply kill someone?

The FBI says it's 450.

Yet there's more to Catherine's commonalities than those related to offenders. The victims provide their own clues to analysts. This is the evolving field of victimology, and it is particularly suited to solve these killings. Catherine and I will dive deeper into victimology later. The ViCAP database relies on victimology more and more to identify murders that look alike and therefore might be the work of the same person. If such similarities are present, investigators focus on the victim characteristics in each distinct killing cluster. It's those victim characteristics that, in death, give those women a voice, maybe for the first time in their abbreviated lives. Together, a collective chorus can cry out, *We were killed by the same man.*

That happened again while I was writing this book. This time, a victim's remains gave the police the name of the person who killed her. Rebecca Landrith, forty-seven, had worked as a model, had been a finalist for Miss Manhattan in 2014, and was a talented violinist. Her killer's name, cell phone number, and email address were on a note in her jacket pocket when her body was discovered in a snowbank near the Mile Run interchange off I-80 in Pennsylvania on February 7, 2021.

That much identifying information is seldom found on a victim; usually the police have no idea at first who the killer is. This time, they had no idea who Rebecca was. She had no ID on her. Police used her fingerprints to identify her.

It took just three days from the discovery of Rebecca's body to find and arrest Tracy Ray Rollins Jr., age thirty. Based on the ejected shell casings and human biological evidence recovered, police determined that Rollins had shot Rebecca twenty-six times when she was inside the sleeper berth of his truck. Security video placed Rollins and Rebecca together on February 4, 2021, at the Pilot Travel Center in Franksville, Wisconsin. On February 6, the trucker and his victim were seen again on video at another Pilot in Austintown, Ohio. The next day, Rebecca was dead.

Rebecca's family showed up in court for Rollins's sentencing. Her mother had some words for the judge. "My daughter was brutally murdered and discarded like a piece of garbage," she said. "You can't replace a child."

Rebecca's mother was right—we can't replace any of the victims in the FBI's HSK Initiative. But just maybe, we can learn how to reduce their numbers. That's what the HSK is about.

Long-haul truckers killing women along our interstates isn't some new phenomenon. In fact, the FBI has evidence of multiple highway serial killings dating back to at least the mid-1990s. And those are just the cases the FBI knows about. The Bureau is certain there are even more. It really wasn't until after the terror attacks of 9/11—after the entire FBI came up for air—that the HSK gained momentum, and that wasn't until late 2003. The fact that hundreds of cases, solved and unsolved, dating back decades qualify for inclusion in this initiative means that history keeps repeating itself.

That's why it's worth looking at some of the oldest cases in the initiative, cases that exemplify what victimology is all about—cases like the Redhead Murders.

She wore a sweater—nothing else. Her body was discovered along I-40 in West Memphis, Arkansas, on September 16, 1984. There were no family members who were searching for her. No one claimed her as their own. It took nine months after she was strangled to finally match her fingerprints to a name. Then a couple from Florida said they had known her; they had let her live with them for a while. Lisa Nichols, from West Virginia, was twenty-eight years old. Some people said they might have seen her at a truck stop, maybe trying to hitchhike.

She had strawberry-blond hair. That would be important later.

Soon after Thanksgiving Day 1984, about two months after Lisa was found, the family of Tina Marie McKenney Farmer, a twenty-one-year-old from Indiana, reported Tina was missing. On New Year's Day 1985, a woman's decomposing body was found wrapped in a blanket, like a macabre present, off Interstate 75 north of Nashville. She had been strangled and had been dead for several days before she was discovered. She was pregnant at the time of her demise. And she had bright red hair.

While it took Arkansas police nine months to identify the remains of Lisa Nichols, it took Tennessee authorities a bit longer to put a name to the body found in their neck of the woods. Thirty-three years longer. They eventually determined it was Tina. But until they did, Tina remained Jane Doe.

On April 1, 1985, the body of another woman was discovered crammed into a refrigerator at a dump site in rural Knox County, Kentucky, just off the Cumberland Gap Parkway. She was between twenty-five and thirty-five and wore two necklaces, one with a heart pendant, one with an eagle. She had on a pair of white socks. That's all—just socks. The medical examiner determined that she'd died of asphyxiation. A couple of witnesses claimed a woman who looked like the victim had been at a truck stop in Corbin, Kentucky, trying to hitch a ride to North Carolina. As with Tina in Tennessee, it took Kentucky police over thirty years to learn the name that belonged to this body. In 2017, DNA results identified the woman as Espy Regina Black-Pilgrim from North Carolina.

Espy had auburn hair.

The deaths of Lisa, Tina, and Espy are considered part of a string of from six to eleven unsolved homicides involving other Jane Does—all reddish-haired petite young women found dead near highways in Tennessee, Kentucky, Arkansas, Pennsylvania,

Ohio, Texas, and Mississippi between 1978 and 1992. These are the Redhead Murders. Since the victims appeared to be transients and were often sex workers, police theorized that the killer was also someone on the move. In 1985, investigators started thinking that the killings were connected. Maybe. They brought together a multistate task force to try and get their arms around whatever it was that was happening.

Cloth torn from Linda Schacke's T-shirt had been stuffed down her throat, just like with Tina Farmer. Linda had freckles and red hair; so did Tina Farmer. It happened on March 5, 1985, just a few months after Tina's murder. Linda got an offer from a customer at the club where she was a dancer. The guy handed Linda a hundred dollars and promised to double that if she had sex with him. They eventually left the club together. The man ripped up Linda's T-shirt, tied her up, and transported his human cargo in her own car into the woods near I-40. He wrapped her T-shirt around her neck and strangled Linda into unconsciousness. Police matched the kind of knot in that T-shirt cloth to the knot in the cloth found around Tina's neck. Linda was left gagged, restrained, and lifeless in a storm drain.

Except Linda wasn't dead. She had pretended. She survived. Linda could identify the guy. This could be the break the cops had looked for, the one that would tie all these heinous crimes together.

If only.

Linda Schacke was able to point police to her attacker. Jerry L. Johns, thirty-six, of Cleveland, Tennessee, was arrested in March 1985 after a hundred-mile-an-hour chase through

Knoxville. The police described Johns as an extremely intelligent ex-con who had taken numerous criminal justice courses and was fascinated by serial killings. Investigators from Kentucky to Texas lined up to talk to Johns about their own cases. But the evidence wasn't there. Try as they might, they simply could not put Johns in their towns, on their highways, for their murders.

In 1987, Johns was convicted in the aggravated assault and kidnapping of Linda. He would die in prison in 2015. Yet his body—specifically his DNA—convicted him of one more crime. In December 2019, thirty-five years after Tina Farmer was murdered, Tina's body would also speak. Detectives were finally able to match Johns's DNA to the sample taken from Tina's remains. A grand jury was assembled, and they announced that they would have indicted Johns in Tina's killing if he were still among the living.

But that was it. After exhaustive investigation and forensic testing, all anyone could say was that Johns had killed Tina and abducted and assaulted Linda. Someone else was out there—maybe a lot of someone elses.

In February 1986, another red-haired woman escaped from yet another driver's rig. Thomas Lee Elkins was charged in Dyer County, Tennessee, after a twenty-year-old bolted out of his truck cab. She told detectives that Elkins had kidnapped and raped her in either Illinois or Indiana, and she'd escaped from his truck when he fell asleep. Police interviewed Elkins about a number of unsolved murders but couldn't link him to those crimes.

On October 26, 2018, Hayes Hickman wrote a well-crafted summary of the Redhead Murders for the *Knoxville News Sentinel*. Hickman made this observation for anyone who might think that it can't be that hard to solve these killings: "Elkins and Johns, however, highlight another alarming aspect of why the so-called Redhead Murders have proven so difficult to solve," he wrote. "They are not uncommon crimes." He's right. Truckers killing women—redheaded or not—isn't unusual. Not at all.

There are at least twenty-five truckers doing prison time for murder. Truckers like Dellmus Colvin, the "Interstate Strangler," who estimates that he murdered between forty-seven and fifty-two women, most of them prostitutes, between 2004 and 2005, though he didn't keep an exact count. Colvin explained that he killed out of pleasure as opposed to sex; he denied having sex with corpses and sometimes laughed during interviews. He said that he'd once answered a phone call from his mother while killing a woman and that he had no regrets about what he'd done. And Colvin disputed what he called a "myth" that when you kill a person who looks directly in your eyes, it will haunt you forever. "I always slept well at night," he said to one interviewer.

Colvin liked to use plastic bags and duct tape—that was his thing. He offered investigators the locations of many of his body-dump sites except those locations that happened to be in death-penalty states. He sits in prison in Lebanon, Ohio, convicted of only seven murders in and around Ohio. "Only" seven. But even if Colvin's estimate was correct and he did kill around fifty women, he couldn't have committed all the unsolved murders. Certainly not the ones that occurred after he was imprisoned.

Much of the quest to solve these cases involves cops and crime analysts. No—scratch that. It doesn't just involve them; it depends on them, on the homicide detectives in city police departments, the deputies in rural county sheriff's offices, the crime analysts for state police agencies. They toil in departments big and small, some with no detectives, some with one or two. Some have heard of ViCAP, and some wouldn't know how to enter their cases in that crucial FBI database if their lives depended on it.

But lives do depend on it—the lives of the next victims.

Catherine and the BAU analysts study victims after they are dead to learn more about who killed them. But what could I learn from the living—a victim who had been trafficked at truck stops, been beaten and abused in those trucks, a survivor, someone like Hannah Everett? It turned out I would learn plenty.

CHAPTER 3

GIRLS NEXT DOOR

The trucker kept beating her. She was desperate and dope sick and certain that her life would end inside that truck. All she thought about was how another girl had been raped, beaten, and tossed unconscious into a field an hour outside of town. She was determined not to be another victim. She shifted into survival mode. In her situation, neither fight nor flight was an option, but she could talk and pretend, so she did.

Something clicked in her brain. She told the driver that the truck-stop cameras must have grabbed a photo of his license plate. She claimed there were friends following her. She said the cops would send him to prison.

She kept talking and screaming and crying. Then she tried another route.

"I'll give you all the money back!"

It worked. The trucker shoved his panicked passenger out the door and onto the frontage road like yesterday's trash.

It was a day in the life of what truckers called a lot lizard. It's what lot lizards called themselves too. If one of them survived that kind of encounter, could she survive them all and find a different life? How does that become someone's life—or death? What does the path of what I call pre-victimization even look like? I needed to understand. I particularly wanted to wrap my mind around how an all-American girl next door—like the woman who is called Hannah in this book—ended up trafficked to truckers. Hannah agreed to meet with me as a consultant; she even signed a release for this book and approved her alias in the hopes that, by telling me her story and about the work she now does, she could provide insights into truckers, trafficking, and victims. More important, she hoped that someone out there might be helped, inspired, maybe rescued by reading this book.

I hit the ground at an airport in the Midwest on Friday around midday and grabbed an Uber for the twenty-minute ride north. In an earlier series of texts, Hannah had agreed to start our multiday conversation with dinner. After she suggested three different options ("Do you have any dietary restrictions or any foods you don't particularly care for?"), we settled on a place that served decent Greek food. In her almost compulsively coordinating, people-pleasing fashion, Hannah had sent me links to three nearby hotels to consider for my lodging. Those efforts at planning and coordinating, smoothing over issues for others, gave me some of my first insights into who Hannah was. Soon I'd learn more. Much more.

Those hotel choices were convenient to the Course Change Center, where Hannah worked in the center's human and sex trafficking support initiative. It's a place designed to offer women the many services they need to turn away from trafficking. It was also where we spent most of our waking hours for the next couple of days, with the permission of its leadership.

Soon after I checked into the worn, dated chain hotel near Hannah's office, she texted me.

Hi, Frank, hope you made it okay. I wanted to reach out because we had a bunch of emergency intakes today, I was hoping to be able to have dinner tonight but it's not looking so good. We just got started on these intakes. I'm not sure if you want me to message you when done. Once I am finished, if it's not too late, I could message you and take it from there?

With twenty-five years in the FBI, I was no stranger to Friday-night emergencies—were there any other kind? It didn't surprise me that the same was true for victim advocacy. It turned out that three women had chosen this Friday evening to flee from the same pimp; they couldn't go another weekend on the street. True to her word, Hannah texted me an update later to confirm dinner wasn't happening. We agreed to meet at eight thirty a.m. the next day. She would pick me up outside my hotel and we'd head to Course Change.

Good morning, I will be leaving in about thirty minutes to pick up coffee. I'll be there at 8:30 a.m. and let you know when I'm about ten minutes away. That was my Saturday-morning text from Hannah.

When I slid into Hannah's Ford sedan, there was an unsolicited venti-size Starbucks waiting for me on the console, a simple gesture that suggested her larger and learned longing to minimize any risk posed by the unknown. I was an unknown. When we walked into the conference room at Course Change, I saw fresh fruit and pastries on the conference table. Had Hannah already been here this morning?

This young lady, in her late twenties with green eyes and a thick mane of brown hair, had grown up in a slumbering, unpretentious village in the north-central Midwest. Her family were hardworking blue-collar folks of European heritage, churchgoing brick masons, millworkers, and cops.

The human-trafficking experts and social workers I consulted for this book taught me that there were specific patterns and commonalities in the lives of victims. Not every young person with this background became a victim, but the existence of one or more of those indicators was frequently found in the personal stories of those who were ultimately trafficked. Elements of their early lives pointed them down a path of vulnerability and, later, victimization. While each of these women had unique stories and circumstances, they had more similarities than differences. Some of the victims' stories contained only a few of the recognized warning signs that foreshadow a descent into destruction. Yet many of the women eventually, sooner or later, experienced most or all the danger signs. Hannah was one of the many.

Some women had early childhood recollections of their parents fighting; some of their parents drank heavily or disappeared for days at a time. There were memories of lots of drunken yelling, arguing, throwing things. The smell of alcohol imprinted on a young mind became the smell of trouble. I was told stories of young siblings huddled in a closet, covering their ears, sobbing, and trying to comfort each other. To the outside world, these families often seemed serene. The grass got mowed; the kids went to school.

In some stories, the appearance of serenity was broken when the police showed up on a domestic call and a parent was arrested. That began the trauma that triggered the need to make things better, to alter the current reality. Tough stuff for little kids; difficult memories for an adult. If only those earliest memories had been the end, not the beginning, of the trauma. In Hannah's case, her mom packed up Hannah and her sibling and trekked to another town. Hannah thought they were going on a road trip, but she soon found out that her parents were divorcing.

So many of the stories that victims shared with me included a traumatizing violation at an early age. One such victim wanted me to know what happened because she felt it was important for people to understand. When the woman reached this part of our discussion, she took a deep breath in and let it out forcefully. She paused. I sensed that talking about this was almost as difficult as experiencing it. It happened one summer when she was still a kid, a preteen.

There was this man in her neighborhood who came around often. One day, her parents were out running an errand. That solitary moment in time was enough for him to steal this little girl's innocence. That's all that needs to be said. She was tricked, traumatized, and twelve.

I was struck by the randomness of this molestation, the seizure of a single moment by an adult predator, the brief window of opportunity that a warped human crawled through. Being hurt like that changes someone's life. If unacknowledged and unaddressed, the trauma lurks just beneath the surface, altering who someone is and who she becomes.

Nancy Yarbrough was a girl next door, a PK—preacher's kid—from Wisconsin. She told her story publicly to the press and in a TEDx talk in Oshkosh, Wisconsin. Nancy's upbringing was filled with love, faith, and a keen sense of right and wrong.

Her homelife exemplified the scripture passage that hangs framed in many Christian homes: "But as for me and my house, we will serve the Lord" (Joshua 24:15). That foundation didn't mean Nancy was immune from the traumas that take girls next door down a trail to trafficking.

The trauma started early. "So, my journey began when I was younger, way younger than I needed to have had somebody touch me inappropriately and not know how to respond. So, my first interaction with being exploited was unwanted touches." People she was familiar with committed acts Nancy was most unfamiliar with. She couldn't imagine how to tell her parents what had happened, so it remained unspoken.

Nancy's parents divorced, and her older brother took on the role of head of the household. It didn't go well. Nancy experienced more trauma, more of the unfamiliar. The personal violations came at the hands of extended-family members. "They took advantage of these vulnerabilities that lie in the heart of any child, of anyone who wants to be loved and accepted." More traumas came at school, where Nancy said her peer group shunned her. She was "bullied, ostracized, teased at school." In her young mind, based on what was happening, Nancy began to view her value, her worth, as something defined by older males driven by their own self-interest. She said that she started turning to men to seek attention and affirmation.

There's a trail of trauma in the lives of trafficking victims. The traumas can start early and then stack up into a tower that crushes and consumes whoever is under it. Victims shared tragic stories of childhoods filled with grief, including the accidental death of close family members, suicides or attempted suicides, major illnesses, and the pain of parents cheating on each other. There were roller-coaster rhythms, times when everything seemed right with the world, followed by dramatic plunges that sent everyone reeling.

Nancy and Hannah experienced the kinds of journeys I needed to learn more about. Hannah had her own personal details that she might share in her own way, in her own time, like Nancy did. Those intimate particulars remain Hannah's to tell, maybe revealing the predators who marked her slow but sure path into darkness. For now, for the purpose of my research, I'm sticking with the generalities of Hannah's story that most mirror the core elements of what others have told me about their journeys.

These shared pathways were split into before and after. Sometimes there was the before and the after of parents' volatile divorce. For some, there was the before and after of childhood molestations. Others noted the before and the after of a tragic death of a beloved relative. Of course, these victims described their stories with the benefit of hindsight, a benefit bestowed only on those who have lived to have that luxury.

Early exposure to drugs was relatively common among some, although not all, of the victims I met. Older siblings, relatives, peers, parents, and certainly aspiring pimps were often responsible for introducing drugs into the picture. There was frequent early-age marijuana use among a trusted group, the weed transforming into a kind of communal sacrament for kids whose developing brains were still under construction.

That was Nancy Yarbrough's reality. She started drinking and using marijuana as a very young kid, substances supplied by older influencers. "That caused me to be raped for the first time, for my first sexual experience."

For these girls next door, the signs of drug use sometimes began to appear in their school performance and at home, but too often the signals were missed by parents distracted by their own traumas, despair, grief, or simply their fight to survive. Teachers and coaches, if they even spotted the indicators, would sugarcoat reality, cut a good kid a break, or assume someone else was addressing the problem. Nancy's parents thought her behavior was merely "teenage rebellion," but she reminded all who might be dealing with similar conduct that "this is not teenage rebellion. I'm crying out. I want help, but nobody notices."

For many victims, drug use served as a salve in a circle of friends who were bonding over their mutual traumas. That bonding sometimes evolved into a romantic relationship between a younger girl and an older teen or man. Since trauma and drugs formed the foundation of the attraction, those same two elements predestined a future filled with more of both. In a typical case, the older partner introduced increasingly harder drugs into the dynamic, often accompanied by pressure and the threat that rejecting the drugs was tantamount to abandoning the relationship. In more than one case, the boyfriend coaxed the girlfriend to partake in the shared pleasure of heroin, assuring her that a small sampling wouldn't lead to addiction. That was always a lie.

Despite declining to use heroin multiple times, some young women eventually caved. They needed to understand this thing that had such power over the men in their life, this substance that won the attention of their partners. One victim told me about the first time she tried heroin: "In a second, my life changed. Anxiety, insecurity, trauma—with heroin, they were gone in seconds."

This next level of drug use also included cocaine, LSD, mushrooms, and ecstasy. Abuse of prescription drugs like OxyContin was prevalent among pre-victims and rampant among those young women who were in the throes of trafficking. Eventually, there was little distinction between dependence on drugs and reliance on the relationship; they were both sources of meaning and affirmation in a life increasingly isolated from the positive influence of family and stable friends.

Victims told me that verbal abuse and physical violence by the male partners were common even in their young, initial relationships. It wasn't unusual for the police to enter the picture in response to domestic disturbances between girlfriend and boyfriend. That influencer/boyfriend often became abusive, in some cases while the girl was still in high school. One young victim I spoke with had been choked by her boyfriend. Another time, he hit her head against furniture. Her attempts to escape the relationship were met with strong opposition, and she was afraid of losing him and her dream of a fairy-tale future. The fear won.

From where I sat, the girls in these budding romantic relationships were the ones who seemed to possess the higher intellect. They also appeared to be more industrious, often working the job, or jobs, that put food on the table. Many young women attended college before finally succumbing to the siren calls of their boyfriends and the drugs. All too often, a victim's hard-earned money was diverted by her partner to purchase drugs. A girl's disbelief upon discovering the frequency and potency of her partner's often secretive drug use was a common theme. But the sense of deceit and betrayal triggered by the revelation that her boyfriend was up to no good seldom resulted in a quick or easy breakup.

The tales about pre-victim pathways were littered with boyfriends' broken promises that they would never again strike them or shoplift or steal; often they pledged to enter and complete drug rehab. You might ask—as I did of Hannah—why these bright, hopeful girls didn't just leave. But at that point, they were isolated from everyone but their boyfriends. The more abusive the men became, the more trapped the women felt. And those boyfriends did indeed become more abusive. In many cases, a type of call-and-response developed: The girlfriend would finally find a way to break off the relationship, only to be lured back by the boyfriend in great need of bail or rent money, companionship, or sustenance. As Nancy noted, the factors that kept her from walking away from predatory men included "fear, vulnerability, and the love we believed we had would now go away."

I was wrong in my preconceived notion that young women involved in trafficking probably came from families who didn't care or who lacked the capacity to do anything about it. Nancy Yarbrough had parents who loved her, provided her with the newest toys and latest fashions. She said that nothing traumatic ever happened within the confines of her home. Some families often tried mightily to create distance between their daughters and dangerous boyfriends. Sometimes it worked temporarily, but often their efforts failed. And sometimes those attempts worked to wipe away the first perilous relationships, but the young women eventually got involved in even more fatal attractions.

Multiple trafficking victims related accounts of early pre-trafficking days when they either looked the other way while a boyfriend or husband committed crimes or outright participated in those crimes. Shoplifting, car theft, and burglary, often to feed a mutual drug habit, further cemented an alluring sense of "us against the world." Becoming partners in crime also fueled a codependent bond and isolation from others. A victim from a law-abiding family described being haunted by anxiety, worrying constantly whether this would be the day the police finally caught up with her or her boyfriend and sent them off to jail. The crimes and the drugs fueled the anxiety, and the anxiety could be quieted only by more drugs. This became an unending cycle, beyond this bad boyfriend and the next one and the one after that, across a developing matrix of drug-addled decision-making, despair, pain, and even jail.

The act of purchasing drugs itself was a source of overwhelming anxiety for girls next door like Hannah. Small towns in the Midwest weren't exactly underworld bazaars brimming with ready supplies of heroin. That meant that kids raised in rural or exurban bubbles who were now hooked like trout on taut lines were reeled into the big city for their next taste. In the upper Midwest, that big city was either Chicago or Detroit. As a young lady described it, you could just drive to a known dealing location in Chicago and wait. "We would take the Cicero exit to Michigan Ave., almost to the lake, and just pull up. A guy comes to your window—that guy doesn't have it, but he whistles to someone who does. Even today, this hasn't changed." The process became routine, and so did the danger-induced dread.

In the span of about a year, a young woman could spiral from occasional drug use to constant craving. Lurking just below the surface of that overwhelming desire was an ever-present fear: Do we get arrested today? Or, worse, robbed and murdered? The relentless anxiety of making the purchase caused one pre-victim to pull over her car and vomit on the way to a purchase. It was a momentary delay of the inevitable score. As usual, the girl and her guy still made their buy. Those fears of arrest or harm were warranted; it was only a matter of time. For so many of these young women, the time grew exponentially closer.

The fate of the girls next door was frequently linked with deeper involvement in drugs, crime, or both. For Nancy, the drug was cocaine. Using drugs and committing crimes were joined at the hip. I met a trafficking victim who explained that she found herself agreeing to hold drugs for her boyfriend, then to hand off heroin to buyers, and then to receive the cash payments. As I listened to these stories, I sensed the train wrecks in progress. A young woman was exploited by the perceived love of her life so he could maintain plausible deniability when the police showed up. Rest assured, the police did eventually arrive. These episodes wouldn't be the last time such women were exploited by a man, or men, for the benefit of everyone but themselves.

The injection of police into the picture sometimes presented an agonizing decision point. Whether detectives were inquiring about narcotics, burglaries, bad checks, or stolen credit cards, they inevitably asked their young defendant to cooperate—to snitch on her boyfriend or on others. In one case, the police proposed that their arrestee engage in controlled buys—drug purchases against specific targets. For the young woman, the fear flooded back: *Do I tell the police what I know? Do I become a rat?* Word travels fast in a small town where everyone knows everything about everyone, including who among them is cooperating with the cops.

Trouble with the law, with family, or with finding work became catalysts for young women like Hannah to catch the wanderlust bug and escape the pressures of the present. Like itinerant farmers seeking greener pastures, off they went with their beaus in rented U-Hauls or old cars groaning with the weight of all their worldly possessions. They road-tripped to warmer climes or to locales where some well-meaning cousin or uncle sang the praises of job opportunities or easier living. Some scraped together all their remaining funds to make the move happen; others pleaded with their parents or relatives and pledged that this move would be the fresh start, the new beginning that would make all the difference in their lives. Hopeful parents, not understanding the depth of the drug use, wanted to believe that geographic distance from the wrong crowd and the drug supply was the answer to their prayers. But miles didn't make miracles.

For some, at first, the freshness of new jobs, a new apartment, maybe the encouragement of a local relative or friend, contributed to a genuine sense that life was looking up. Hannah told me tales typical of addicts who swore to stop using—the "just one more time" phenomenon, a splurge on one last binge before hitting the gas pedal and magically leaving addiction behind. Blowing wads of cash, often provided by moms or dads, on copious quantities of heroin or Oxy or both was a form of self-sabotage that undermined the best of intentions. The last-minute binges became part of a "wash, rinse, repeat" pattern over months or years of drug-induced stupors, failed stints in rehab, and multiple relocations aimed at more fresh starts, all of which quickly became old news.

Hannah and Nancy certainly weren't the only young ladies from Midwest towns to experience heartache and trauma. Trauma had visited twenty-nine-year-old Sharon Kay Hammack long before Hannah was born. In August 2022, twenty-six years after a citizen made the unpleasant discovery of a woman's remains rolled up in a blanket near Grand Rapids, Garry Dean Artman was finally caught and charged for murdering Hammack. Sharon had been bound by her hands and feet, raped, and stabbed. Hammack, a mother of two, was an addict and had engaged in prostitution, just like twelve or so other women found dead near Grand Rapids during the 1990s. A long-hauler, Artman had a record of violence, including a rape conviction that sent him to prison in Michigan for nearly a dozen years.

Like so many other victims', Sharon Hammack's corpse spoke for her, pointing to her killer. Unfortunately, it took two and a half decades for someone to get the message. Hammack's vagina and rectum contained traces of Artman's DNA, as did the rope used to bind her. Detectives submitted that DNA and waited.

In 2006, Maryland State Police provided to their laboratory the DNA from the body of a murdered sex worker who had also been raped. That DNA matched the DNA from Hammack's case in Michigan and revealed the murderer was responsible for both deaths. Now the police needed to know who that person was. The rapidly advancing field of forensic genealogical testing came to the rescue.

Using publicly available DNA databases, police traced the DNA to the parents of four sons. Only one son was connected to Michigan. Garry Artman had lived and worked near the Hammack murder scene, and police could place him within twenty miles of the Maryland victim.

I couldn't possibly access all the case files or meet all the women who, like Hannah, Nancy, and, tragically, Sharon Kay Hammack, became trafficking victims, but I could find someone who knew a multitude of Hannahs, Nancys, and even Sharons.

CHAPTER 4

THE PIONEER PROFESSOR

"Therapists don't understand that trauma is the root cause."

That's what Dr. Celia Williamson told me. She knows a thing or two about street-level and truck-stop sex work. In 2021, Dr. Williamson was named among the top thirty most influential social workers for her research and community advocacy in the fight against human trafficking and prostitution. A distinguished professor of social work at the University of Toledo and director of the Human Trafficking and Social Justice Institute, Williamson founded Ohio's first anti-trafficking program in 1993. Williamson's passion for her mission led her to start the Second Chance program (later called RISE), which won the FBI director's Community Leadership Award in 2009; initiate the Lucas County Human Trafficking Coalition; and serve as a founding member and president of the Global Association of Human Trafficking Scholars.

For twenty-eight years, Williamson has written and taught extensively about the sex trafficking of minors and about adult prostitution in America. She also has a podcast called *Emancipation Nation*, dedicated to combating sex trafficking. Naturally, I wanted to speak with Dr. Williamson, and she graciously shared her time with me.

"Truck-stop and street-level prostitution has its own culture, its own language, and its own processes," she explained. Williamson described for me the commonalities within this culture that apply to both the street corner and the truck stop. Clearly, drugs are one common experience, at least at some point along the journey. So are similar childhood experiences, including some form of molestation or abuse and estrangement from a parent or family.

There's a unique language of the sex trade that facilitates conversation about goods and services without direct reference to what's really happening. It has its own cryptic code. The terminology is so pervasive among hookers, pimps, and truckers that it wasn't long before it was widely known to cops, anyone with a CB radio, and researchers like Dr. Williamson.

For example:

House refers to a tractor trailer, as in "I'm in the bright red house."

Lot lizards is what truckers call sex workers at truck stops— certainly not a term of endearment.

Trick is a trucker who seeks the services of a lot lizard.

Bottom is a prostitute who functions like a deputy to a pimp, a kind of sergeant who monitors, mentors, and helps maintain control over the women who work under the pimp. A bottom might walk a girl into a truck cab to ensure a transaction is properly negotiated and the girl isn't trying to escape.

Stable refers to the pimp's cadre of prostitutes, as in "I have eight women in my stable."

Out of pocket refers generally to when a girl in a stable breaks any of her pimp's many rules, like trying to distance herself from her pimp or bottom, working for herself or another pimp, or temporarily disappearing.

Shorty is a slang term for an attractive female, girlfriend or sex worker, popularized by rappers. A pimp might say, "My shorty is working hard tonight." In fact, *shorty* has wormed its way into popular culture and is widely used instead of *girlfriend*.

Dr. Williamson's work is far more to her than an academic pursuit. It's personal. She shared her own story of her troubled youth and a childhood spent in a gritty section of Toledo: "One of my friends was murdered. That friend was one of three trafficked girls. My friend was murdered by her trick."

Celia Williamson could have been that girl, but for some reason she is still around to help women avoid the fate of her young friend.

As a kid, the professor tried selling marijuana, and she acquired enough weed to set out on her own and start dealing. She had big plans, but those plans ended before they even began: "I was robbed during my first attempted sale."

Celia Williamson was meant to do other things, like understand the world of trafficking so deeply that she helps some victims escape.

Knowing my law enforcement background, the professor thought I'd be interested in hearing how the man who murdered her friend was caught. She was right; I was interested.

"That trick was driving his own mother's car. Before the killing, he shopped at Walmart and had kept his receipt inside the car. When my murdered friend was found, she had a Walmart receipt clinging to her back. That receipt led police to the murderer." He is still in prison today.

A young girl for sale—found with a receipt of purchase on her back.

Truck stops are where the action is because that's where the demand is, Dr. Williamson said. Supply flowed to match the demand. "Everyone is going to the truck stop. It's the girls' bread and butter. They can make two to three thousand a night there. The bottom will want to go sit in the truck with the pimp-controlled girl to make sure she gets the job done and to ensure she gets the money."

As I spoke with Professor Williamson, I could clearly see the perfect storm of variables that converged when a perfect victim (a sex worker) encountered a perfect predator (a trucker intent on rape, kidnapping, or murder). Williamson emphasized the power disparity between a working girl and a murderous trucker. The trucker sits atop hulking machinery, wallet filled with cash, able to hit the highway in an instant. He is "looking for women with no power."

The trucker finds his perfect prey in that girl who is either high on drugs or needs to get high soon; a girl who needs cash, wants a meal, fears the police, fled her family, feels nothing but pain or feels nothing at all. As Williamson describes it, it's a match made in hell.

In her nearly three decades orbiting the planet of prostitution, Williamson doesn't see much change in the truck-stop trafficking culture. She cautioned against perceiving drops in activity in certain places at certain times as evidence that prostitution in the trucking industry has waned. Transient, anonymous men with little or no accountability continue to fuel the demand side of the illicit economic equation. As long as that demand exists, transient, anonymous girls and women will provide the supply side of the transaction.

Williamson explained that any tangible lessening in street and truck-stop sex trade is part of an ebb and flow related to community awareness. A community becomes aware of the problem, perhaps because of an incident, and that places pressure on the police to enforce the law. But it's cyclical.

Humanitarian and activist groups often learn of a specific threat or risk in a certain area long before the police know what is happening. So Williamson often made working girls aware of the latest intelligence about somebody or something that posed a concern. Flyers were distributed that advised *Don't get into this blue car* or *Watch out for this guy*.

While she concedes that a "murder might be taken seriously" by the police, Dr. Williamson knows from experience that even when a working girl gathers enough strength to report something, it isn't unusual for a police officer to "stop writing" when he realizes what the girl does for a living or the nature of what she's reporting.

Then Williamson said the quiet part out loud: "You know, police participate as well."

Which means, of course, that it is certainly not unheard of for officers to pay, or not pay, for the services of trafficked victims or to abuse those women or even worse. Dr. Williamson provided more for me to ponder when she asked me what sounded like a rhetorical question: "Should a male-dominated police force even be investigating such things?"

I prompted the professor to help me with the question of whether it might be possible to predict which trafficked women are more likely to be murdered by their clients. Does Dr. Williamson's social work research offer insights into the crime analysts' concept of victimology? Though this wasn't her objective, it turns out that Williamson's research holds some answers.

Dr. Williamson partnered with Dr. Lynda M. Baker of Wayne State University in Detroit to research an area that few other sex-industry analysts focused on—the varying work styles of street prostitutes. As part of their study, Williamson and Baker interviewed fifty-three adult women in the Midwest, including some who had plied their trade at truck stops. Twenty-one of those women started selling themselves before they turned eighteen. For any researcher or social worker who previously viewed street-level prostitutes as essentially all the same and therefore treatable in the same way, Williamson and Baker's research became a kind of master class on multiple realities.

The research confirms three basic approaches to working the nation's streets and truck stops: pimp-controlled, renegade, and outlaw. Although clear categorization is tough because women sometimes start in one category, try another, then maybe slip into the third, they often stick with what they know. This is important stuff, not just for social workers but for someone like me trying to understand who is killing and who is being killed. Important, too, because learning how a woman works a truck stop might shed light on how, or whether, she survives the truck stop.

Twelve of the fifty-three women in Dr. Williamson's study were pimp-controlled. These women spoke their own kind of code, which included terms like *wife-in-laws, quota, being turned out, becoming a thoroughbred, choosing up,* and *being out of pocket.* The majority of pimp-controlled women said their entry into trafficking didn't involve physical force. Instead, they were "enticed, finessed, and manipulated as adolescents into a work style they believed would either be exciting and bring them material success and mobility or help them survive the harsh conditions of street life." Sometimes the pimp himself would do the recruiting; other times he would delegate the job to other women or to male associates on his team.

Williamson and Baker found there was an orientation phase in which the women were indoctrinated into the practice and protocols of prostitution. Often, this mentoring was the work of wife-in-laws. In this dark domain, wife-in-laws are the more trusted girls in the pimp's stable, girls who have the additional duty of closely monitoring and maintaining the pimp's other girls.

"I had about six wife-in-laws. We had to do what we had to do. We was with the same man so we had to get along, because if we didn't get along, he would jump us or whatever. He would check us. And, you know, he's like 'Bitch, you gotta do this. Bitch you better go out today.' Because he's supposed to be your pimp. You got wife-in-laws and stuff and you better go do it." That was Brenda, a pimp-controlled woman in Williamson's study.

Professor Williamson discovered that women experienced in prostitution were known as thoroughbreds and were expected to handle customers without much supervision. They were turned out onto the streets to meet a quota determined by the pimp. For example, one woman, Joan, was expected to make $250 at one truck stop, while for Mara, the amount was much higher. Mara told the researchers: "Well, when I started off, when I first got with him, the first place he took me was to

Miami, Florida. The quota that we had to bring in that night was at least $800. If we didn't have that quota, it wasn't about no coming in. It was about being out there until you did get it."

Dr. Williamson found there was no way for women to only partially accept their relationships with their pimps. A pimp-controlled girl either accepted that she was wholly owned and operated—financially, physically, and mentally—by her pimp, or she was cast to the wind and left to fend for herself. The study noted, "If a woman becomes unhappy with her current pimp, she can choose up, meaning choose another pimp to control her business. In a kind of ritual, the girl has to place money in the new pimp's hand to confirm the choose-up."

If a woman chose another player, "the money that you give him buys the protection you need. If your other pimp try to come up on you, he won't be able to touch you because you been done paid this other man to be with him. Because the other pimp will tell the other one that she chose me. She paid me so she with me now." That was Mary, who was pimp-controlled.

In what could be the saddest of ironies, it is the 24/7 control of the pimp that, despite the beatings, the drugs, and the mental abuse, oddly enough offers a form of protection from outsiders. If someone—a pimp, a bottom, or a wife-in-law—is always watching, maybe a woman is less likely to be killed or abducted by one of her tricks. Or, maybe not. I wasn't sure yet.

Because choosing up is an option for an unhappy trafficked woman, pimps have to balance their approach between terror and tenderness. A pimp has to instill enough fear to keep his women from squandering their hard-earned money on themselves yet remain alluring enough that women think they cannot walk away from him. While choosing up is allowed, a trafficking victim who goes off on her own or completely jettisons sex work finds herself in another kind of trap. Clawing her way out of that trap often entails a dramatic high-risk escape. Williamson shared this insight from Linda:

"It was for any little thing, he'd slap me. One time he was whooping me with a coat hanger. But I'm physically . . . I couldn't whoop him, but mentally, see he didn't go to school. I mentally . . . I could think and I was like, if you hit me with that who's going to buy me? Look at me. There's no way I'm going to let you do that to me . . . But he still, he kept me in line, and in control. But he beat me up one time and I ran away and went with some other people."

As a part of this work style, women are forced to follow the rules of their pimp and are physically abused if they violate them. A pimp-controlled woman named Carol stated, "He beat the living shit out of me. He beat me severely. I had to have surgery done on my legs. I had to have an artificial knee due to him and surgery on my ankle. He took a 2x4 to me. And that's how he disciplined me. He would make me cross my legs and have another man hold my legs together while he smacked me with the 2x4."

Carol, interviewed as part of Williamson and Baker's study, was squarely in the pimp-controlled category of street-girl work styles. So too was Carla, another prostitute who agreed to be interviewed as part of the two professors' research.

"It's been times when the money wasn't right. And when I

come in at night, I had to sleep naked. No blanket, no clothes, cold. You staying in a hotel and the bed be warm, and I just be on the floor freezing."

Professor Williamson found that a pimp could attempt to entice any woman away from another pimp. In fact, this is viewed as a component of free enterprise. However, to control the women in their stable, most professional pimps establish rules preventing their women from making eye contact with other pimps or engaging another pimp in conversation. To do so is considered *reckless eyeballing,* a term signifying the potential loss of pimp revenue and another form of being out of pocket. The consequence is often physical violence.

Sandra described the ramifications of eye contact. "And if you cut your eyes at another player, you get slapped. You get tore up." Withholding money or leaving the "ho stroll" early are also examples of being out of pocket.

Addiction is the engine that keeps the car moving, and the pimp is in the driver's seat. A pimp decides how much of that engine's power he wants to use. Williamson found that the more professional a pimp, the less likely his women were to engage in drug use. The less professional pimps were likely to abuse drugs right alongside their women. For some pimps, the foundation of the trafficking enterprise was built on the women's capacity to earn cash to purchase drugs. Women reported to Williamson that their pimps allowed them to smoke marijuana or drink socially only after their work had ended. Mary had to adhere to specific rules concerning drug and alcohol use: "You just go into bars. You couldn't drink while you were working. You couldn't smoke no weed while you was working. All that type of stuff. It was just strictly about the money."

"It's not a pleasant experience for a girl to put her face in the lap of a trucker who's been driving for ten hours."

That was Professor Williamson making certain I understood that regardless of the type of pimp a trafficked woman works for, they always lived at the weak base of a power vortex, surrounded by the controlling swirl of pimp, bottom, dope, and trick. Message received.

Just as truck-stop prostitutes have differing work styles, so do their pimps. There are two widely recognized categories of pimps: finesse and guerrilla. Those labels pretty much speak for themselves. Dr. Williamson emphasizes that in some ways, the two categories of pimps might be a distinction without a difference. "Pimping is about power and control over women. The different labels simply describe how that control is exerted."

Control and coercion figure prominently in this business, whether the control is from a pimp, a drug addiction, or the lure of cash.

Finesse pimps see themselves as smarter and savvier than their guerrilla counterparts. The finesse pimp gives a girl her vision, even if it's a far cry from her reality. They even refer to that relationship in royal terms. The women are told they are "queens," and the pimp is their "king." For many of the victims, this twisted fantasy is often the first taste of affection and self-worth they've ever experienced.

The finesse pimp controls his stable with a royal fantasy of

king and queens; the guerrilla pimp controls through pure un-
adulterated fear. Fear of the next beating. Fear of the next verbal lashing. Fear of what will happen on the street without the
security the pimp provides. Fear of where their next meal, their
next pair of shoes, their next rush from crystal meth will come
from. Fear that they are utterly worthless without their pimp.

Ironically, even though hundreds of unsolved murders appear to be the handiwork of truckers, working a truck stop offers
a prostitute at least an illusion of security that isn't always available when working the street. Often when getting into a car, the
woman must direct her trick to a designated date spot—a dark
alley or other secluded place. On the plus side, she knows that
spot; she's used it before; it works for her. On the downside, if
she is going to be the victim of violence there, no one will hear
her screams.

The truck stop seems different. The entire sex transaction
occurs in the cab of the truck without it ever leaving its parking
space. There are other trucks around, and maybe a gas station
and a restaurant—how dangerous can it be?

"Very dangerous" is the short answer. The longer answer often depends on at least three variables. First is how close the
pimp-controlled prostitute is to making her mandated quota for
the day. That's because risk avoidance becomes a cost-benefit
equation when the night is ending and funds are low. Second is
the loss of judgment associated with the inevitable impairment
of drugs or alcohol. That impairment isn't an "if"; it's a "when."

As Dr. Williamson emphasized, "Nearly all these women
will eventually become drug-addicted."

The third variable is the degree to which mental illness impedes a woman's capacity to lower the odds of transitioning from trafficking victim to murder victim.

Dr. Williamson says the women she studied developed very elaborate street-survival skills and instincts that rivaled those of experienced street cops and FBI veterans like me. She calls those skills "chatting and checking" behaviors. In fact, Williamson discovered that those powers of observation seem stronger than those of the best social workers.

"As social workers, we learn to assess people, we observe human behaviors, but the best at that are women on the street. When they walk up to a car or truck, they make an immediate assessment. *Is this guy going to hurt me? Does he really want to pay money for sex? Does he have a knife hidden between his legs? In his pocket?*"

It's all part of quickly answering, many times a day, a potentially life-and-death question—"Is this a date I will take?" Williamson explained.

"The women do all this while simultaneously scanning the area for the police. They then do the same thing as they exit the vehicle"—another vulnerable time, the professor added. In fact, after could be more dangerous than before, because after was when the women were holding money, which meant that they could—and did—get robbed.

It isn't surprising then that these women extend their risk-mitigation techniques beyond the before and after to also include the during. Pimps, bottom girls, or more seasoned prostitutes teach newbies to constantly calculate a quick escape. Women told Williamson what their escape strategy looked like when they were performing oral sex, facedown, proned out, across the front seats of a car or the cab of a truck. Williamson learned that "during a blow job, while in the passenger side of the vehicle, she places her left foot toward the middle of the front floor panel, her right foot near the car door, her right hand near the door handle, and keeps her left hand free to punch him in the face."

What the professor describes is indeed akin to an FBI agent assessing a high-risk scenario, on the street or undercover, processing a multitude of variables to ensure he or she goes home that night in one piece. The women also share risk strategies to deal with the pandemic-level threat of sexually transmitted disease. Many of their clients often insist on not using a condom. But Williamson explained the girls had "a whole system to slip on a condom without him knowing."

We talked about survival skills, and we also discussed the factors that erode or even erase those skills. Dr. Williamson— the consummate clinician and academic—referenced what social workers called the "ninety symptoms of trauma," including drug use. The pairing of drugs and trauma is pervasive in street-level sex.

"Eventually, all the women get access to drugs, and all the women have trauma. Over time, all their survival instinct and wariness go out the door. Crack highs last no more than ten minutes so they need more tricks, to get more money, to buy more crack."

Being high or needing to get high leads trafficked women to miss all the signs of danger. Women told Williamson stories of judgment so impaired that, unexplainably, "they allowed tricks they had never met to duct tape their ankles."

Another trafficking victim told Williamson about smoking crack, naked, with a trick in a motel on Telegraph Road in Toledo. He beat her, punched her on the bed until she couldn't feel the punches anymore. The woman recalled hoping she would just "go quickly"—die without feeling it. But as soon as she had that thought, something inside her head said, *You're not going to die today*. She kicked the guy, struggled to get out the door, and crawled away on the gravel drive, knees bloodied. Her date fled to his car and drove off.

Drug addiction and the need for cash to score the next high means a prostitute is more likely to take on brand-new customers—the great unknown, with greater unknown risks. And as indicated in Dr. Williamson's findings, the drug of choice at truck stops and other trafficking marketplaces is perhaps the greatest judgment eroder of all—methamphetamine. It doesn't help, as Dr. Williamson asserts, that "truckers were notorious meth users."

Dr. Williamson found that, along with the crushing pressure of earning the night's cash quota and the fog of drug use, mental health is a major factor contributing to victimization. She is convinced that if these women don't have mental and physical trauma when they enter their work, they soon acquire it. Mental illness increases the risk environment not only by clouding the senses but by altering the mind into believing that the pimp is the only possible source of affection and protection and that it is somehow possible to beat the odds and survive on the streets forever.

Those same three factors—mental illness, drug addiction, and money—explain why it seems like there are no families

demanding answers when women become victims of the ultimate violence, murder. When your mother, your grandmother,
and your sister are fed up with you stealing from them, tired of
the repeated arrests and requests for bail money, emotionally
exhausted from one ruined holiday screaming session after another, and despondent over repeatedly failed attempts at rehab,
inevitably they say, "I can't do this anymore; I have got to let
you go."

Dr. Williamson called this "systematic separation and dis-
tancing." For many of the ultimate victims, that family separation happened well before their demise.

"So what works?" I asked the good professor. She shared
her insights from decades of experience and from learning what
doesn't work.

"Systems often do things the wrong way. The women must
work with people who destigmatize what they've done. They
must be equipped to build boundaries and healthy relationships. The majority have mental-health issues and eventually
drug addiction. Rape is pervasive, as is the trauma that goes
with it." The women may get into some well-intended agency
or organization that claims "We respect women" yet signals
"But not you—you're the scourge of the earth." Even in drug
treatment they won't disclose their prostitution because of the
stigma attached. They are disproportionately women of color
and LGBT.

The professor doesn't pull any punches or pretend it's easy to
defeat the demons that ensnare women in trafficking or to heal
the wounds from that enslavement. It takes repeated, consistent
work to slowly build trust with the victim. Nobody claims high

success rates. It's often one step forward and two steps back. Dr. Williamson's work involves what social workers call a wrap-around approach. It's a decentralized, holistic concept with a wide variety of participating community components, led by a care coordinator.

"When we find a victim, we come around them. We help them make their medical or therapy appointments, give them vouchers for what they needed—diapers, baby formula, rent. If they needed it, we supplied it to help remove the incentive to return to that life," Williamson explained. Eventually, with time and demonstrated progress, grants and resources were provided for school or training. It was a winding, circuitous route to recovery, a laboriously long haul.

Professor Williamson is the OG—the "original gangster"—a respected veteran in the niche field of sex-trafficking social work. She has been there, done that.

Now I needed her equivalent in long-haul trucking. Someone who had driven there, hauled that. Someone like Dale Weaver.

CHAPTER 5

OLD-TIMER

My journey with young Mike would provide a firsthand look at the current state of trucking and the kind of person in the driver's seat now and into the near-term future. Mike embodied the Spirit of Trucking Present and a glimpse of the Spirit of Trucking Yet to Come, but I also needed an encounter with the Spirit of Trucking Past. I found him haunting a modular home park in Glendale, Arizona, on a hot early-autumn day.

Dale Weaver long-hauled for forty years. You name the truck, he'd driven it. Name the load, he'd hauled it. He'd been to all the states in the continental U.S. and to Canada—and almost to Alaska. He said he drove until the pavement ended in St. John, British Columbia; it was just mud after that. "If you go, go in the winter," he advised.

I asked Dale when he first thought trucking was an option for him.

"I grew up in rural Maine. I was eleven, working in the hayfields. I knew I didn't want to do that all my life. I was a tall kid, but very skinny—I couldn't lift the hay bales. I started driving a gravel truck as soon as I was old enough."

In a 2021 piece for NeuroscienceNews.com titled "The Preferred Jobs of Serial Killers and Psychopaths," researcher Michael

Arntfield, a professor and participant in the Murder Account-ability Project, placed truckers among the most represented professions of known serial killers throughout history. Not accountants, not farmers—truckers. Dale Weaver represented a part of that history.

The nation was immersed in the Vietnam War when Dale turned twenty-one. The guys he knew who were drafted didn't come back alive. So Dale decided the best way to avoid the draft and death was to volunteer and enlist. He joined the navy, and he liked it. At first, he requested submarines, with their months of silent, subsurface skulking—the navy's equivalent of long-hauling. But, Dale lamented, "They said I wasn't smart enough." Instead, Dale worked on the flight deck of the USS *Enterprise*. He served three years plus one year of inactive reserves and fulfilled his obligation.

After the navy, Dale moved to Phoenix. But he couldn't get a job there—you had to be in the union even to drive a truck. So he moved to Texas, a nonunion state. A friend from the navy lived in the Dallas–Fort Worth area and offered to let Dale stay with him. Dale got a job right away with Wales Transportation. He drove flatbeds and hauled loads of concrete pipe used in construction projects and in the oil industry. Dale spent five or six years with that company.

Wales let Dale buy his own truck, the dream of many a trucker. But it was a case of "Be careful what you wish for." Wales wouldn't help Dale maintain his truck. He started losing money just with the upkeep. Dale realized that the company had dumped an old truck on its driver and walked away from the cost of maintaining an aging vehicle. When his truck started to break down as it maxed out on miles, Dale couldn't afford to stay at Wales.

Dale put 500,000 miles on that truck, which was a lot back then. Today's trucks are better, higher-quality products that last longer—for example, Dale's last truck racked up 1.6 million miles. That one was a 1996 model that already had 300K miles on it when he bought it.

"If you're buying your own truck today, the odds are stacked against you. It's simply too expensive a proposition for an individual. You better have at least twenty thousand dollars in the bank before you buy your own rig. The big companies have resources you can't dream of having. Those big players even lease the tires on their trucks—they don't buy them outright; they're too expensive. The big boys buy their gas on discounted annual contracts. It's a volume game, so the more trucks and routes a company has, the easier it is to leverage that volume into lower operating costs. A guy can't do that by himself."

Dale's "been there, done that" in the universe of potential truck and load types. Trucks move over 72 percent of our country's freight, and Dale was responsible for more than his fair share of that. He hauled flatbeds, lowboys, refrigerated reefers, giant earthmovers, and tankers filled with oxygen, argon, and nitrogen. The oxygen supplied hospitals; the nitrogen was used in fracking by the Halliburton corporation. Dale saw them dump twenty to thirty truckloads of nitrogen into an oil well. His repertoire expanded from nitrogen to nutrition when he hauled milk. One job had him transport milk from one side of a processing plant to the other side, half a mile away, where they turned it into cheese. He did those runs fifteen or twenty times a night.

We've all seen the escorted loads on the highway, the ones with the trail cars warning of WIDE LOAD AHEAD or OVERSIZE LOAD. Dale's done those too. He hauled escorted loads with a pole car up ahead (it was called a pole car because it literally had a pole on it, fifteen feet tall) and a trail car in the rear. The pole car stayed well out in front of Dale so that if its pole smacked the overpass, the driver would radio back that Dale wasn't going to make it through there.

Not surprisingly, Dale has encountered some trouble along the way. He was parked at a truck stop and heard a guy getting shot just two or three trucks over. It was a robbery. The thief had followed a driver on foot out of the restaurant and forced his way into the cab when the trucker unlocked the door. What the robber didn't know was that the driver had a partner in the sleeper berth. That partner heard the commotion and shot the robber—who also had a gun. There was a big police response that kept Dale and everyone else locked down for hours inside the perimeter of the crime scene.

"I've spent a lifetime at truck stops," Dale told me without any exaggeration. "They've evolved over the years. I used to get my salary sent to me via Western Union. Today, there are WUs at truck stops. But back then, often you'd have to find the WU downtown or someplace else that you couldn't bring your rig. So sometimes I'd park my trailer at a truck stop, detach the trailer, and bobtail to the WU in just my truck cab. It was a nightmare."

Dale couldn't stomach what he called "truck-stop bullshit."

He kept to himself at truck stops. He would sit quietly in the corner of the restaurant and watch the truckers he referred to as "scraggly bastards—who hadn't shaved for days—brag about how many prostitutes they picked up. Their trucks looked as bad as they did."

My old-timer Dale spent a lot of time in Tennessee. He confirmed that the peak era for prostitution at truck stops seemed to be the 1970s and into the early 1980s. He said a trucker was "guaranteed action at truck stops in the seventies." Dale would hear the girls all the time on the CB radio. "Hey, guys, want a date?" they'd broadcast. But usually, they were just right there in the lot.

"You might see a pimp at the truck-stop restaurant. He'd drop off a girl, and she'd work the lot for the night until she earned whatever he demanded of her." There was a lot of this in Tennessee off I-40, Dale said. Terre Haute, Indiana, was a hotbed too. "The lot lizards would climb up on the passenger side of your truck because they could get a better view into the sleeper berth and see if you were really sleeping." In fact, he said, after midnight in Tennessee, they'd beat on your door if they hadn't yet earned their quota.

When Dale sold his own Kenworth truck in 1994 or '95, he took six months off the road. "When you're on the road for months at a time, you have to take this kind of time off or you won't last."

After that respite, Dale tried his best—he really did—to drive for one of the biggest of the big trucking companies, Werner. He lasted two weeks. They had him on a Nebraska-to-Houston route, but it seemed like the world of company trucking had transitioned to digital technology while Dale was driving his own rig. The whole electronic log thing might as well have been brain surgery. He couldn't figure it out or keep up with it. "It's all computers now. Today, long-hauling is all about tech. Cameras, sensors—they know if you're going too fast, if you hit the brakes too hard. All of that sends alerts to whoever you're working for," he told me.

Since Dale struggled with the logs, tracking, and digital documentation, Werner had him call in two or three times a day. Dale was an ultra-experienced driver, certainly not used to being babysat by a bean counter on the other end of a phone. He couldn't take it anymore. One day in 2014, with an empty truck, Dale called his corporate bosses and told them, "I don't care if you don't have a load for me—get me back home to Phoenix." They told Dale they didn't have a job that would take him to Phoenix. Dale replied, "Well, find one or not, I'm going to be leaving your truck in Phoenix." That's just what he did.

Dale wasn't done with trucking, and trucking wasn't done with him. There were still bills to pay and still—to my surprise—types of trucking Dale hadn't tried. Most recently, Dale hauled U.S. mail between postal-distribution centers in Utah and Tucson, Arizona. Transporting big loads of mail was deadline-driven, not unlike driving a rig filled with fresh produce. You had fifteen minutes on either side of your scheduled pickup and off-load times, and if you didn't make it, they wouldn't be able to hold open the assigned loading-dock door for you. "You had better call them if you're going to be late too," he noted.

And to make it worse, all of it was night driving. That's when our mail moves. Dale hauled the mail until he was seventy-four, then called it quits. Most truckers are between forty-five and fifty-four, but a surprising 7 percent are sixty-five or older. Dale said his brain didn't want to do it anymore. He also knew that his required physical was coming up, and he didn't think that would go well. Dale turned in his CDL and traded it for a regular license. Keeping his CDL meant passing mandatory physicals. No physical, no CDL.

Dale was seventy-nine when I spoke to him. He'd recently had a triple bypass and wasn't supposed to lift over twenty or thirty pounds. The surgery cost over $350,000, and Dale battled with the Veterans Administration for four months before they paid a dime of it. The VA said Dale hadn't gotten their permission for the procedure. Dale was incredulous. "How am I supposed to get permission when I'm having a heart attack at three a.m. in the morning? I called the ambulance, which, by the way, the VA never paid for. They don't treat vets like they want everybody to think they do."

The introverted, soft-spoken Dale started to open up. It took several hours of discussion for this to happen.

Dale saw a lot of drug use by drivers in his time. He never did coke or meth, but he did use these little black-and-red capsules that guys sold in jars, like candy, at truck stops. They always had RJS stamped on them. Dale said they were like speed or diet pills that kept you up for twenty-four hours straight, and they were everywhere. The RJS capsules lofted you high, then laid you out like a boxer knocked flat on the canvas. Yes, you could drive for twenty-four hours, but then came an inevitable crash that put you down for days. It just wasn't worth it. Dale found he could make more miles without them.

Dale swore off black-and-red capsules after he and a couple of guys hauled a well casing from west Texas to the Pittsburgh area. They drove nonstop for two and a half days. His truck mates had jars of RJSs and shared them with Dale. He couldn't fall asleep for four days. When Dale finally did fall asleep, he didn't wake up for twenty-four hours. Dale's sojourn into slumber was so profound that he peed the bed and didn't know it. "I never took another pill after that."

RJS capsules were a big deal in the 1970s. On the street, they were black mollies or black beauties. In a laboratory, they were amphetamines. In 1972, the *New York Times* called them the "most popular" black-market drug in America. Manufactured in Mexico for New York drugmaker Strasenburgh Pharmaceuticals, the capsules packed the punch of ten milligrams each of amphetamine and dextroamphetamine. The producer was so proud of the product that it stamped the initials of its founder, R. J. Strasenburgh, on every capsule. The stimulants went for a dollar fifty each in the United States, but if you purchased them across the border in Juarez, you might get them for as little as twenty-five cents apiece. In 1971 alone, a million pills a month made it across the border.

"Truckers combined RJS with vodka, which somehow kept them going even longer. I know it doesn't make sense, but that's what they did," Dale said.

Fifty percent of the 3.5 million American drivers with a CDL must be tested for substance use every year. A recent U.S. DOT Drug and Alcohol Clearinghouse report shows spikes in the use of the most common illegal drugs by truckers, with an almost 13 percent increase overall. In case you're wondering how many

CDL holders barreling by you on the freeway flunked their mandatory drug tests, the answer is over 72,000. That number represents more than 4 percent of tested drivers found to have methamphetamine, cocaine, marijuana, or other prohibited drugs in their systems. The increase in positive drug tests year over year tells us there's a problem. But these DOT stats don't tell us what to do about it.

A 2023 report by American Addiction Centers found that "U.S. truckers had the highest frequency of positive alcohol tests in the world." Ninety-one percent of truckers told interviewers they regularly consumed alcohol, and 27.6 percent admitted to using illegal substances, including amphetamines and cocaine. Nearly 10 percent of truckers reported drinking every day and almost 20 percent said they binge drank five or more drinks in a short period. One study found that 44 percent of long-haul truckers reported symptoms of depression in the previous twelve months. I'd say 100 percent of us should be concerned about how all of this affects everyone's health and safety on the road.

Based on those stats, it was no surprise when Dale had something more to share with me. Something he wanted me to know. He hadn't escaped his own demons.

"I'm an alcoholic. I have to have at least three drinks every night since I retired from trucking. I knew this would happen. I predicted it. That's why it took me so long to retire—I was trying to avoid this. I was highly disciplined when I was driving. Now I have nothing and no one to be disciplined for. When I was driving, I drank only on my downtime, but now it's every night."

I wondered if Dale's story was typical of most veteran long-haul truckers or if I had stumbled on a guy who ticked all or some of the boxes on a crime analyst's HSK checklist: Loner, inability to maintain relationships, substance abuser, disdain for corporate trucking, gun owner. If Dale was typical, I could see a crime analyst's dilemma—too many suspects in too many places. I also wondered, as I looked at Dale, whether I was looking at Mike's future.

CHAPTER 6

MONDAY WITH MIKE

We are up. Groggy, but awake. It was a long, short night. Mike snored and farted in his sleep, which didn't help matters. He tells me it's time to inspect the truck before we launch. We both climb down—more of a controlled fall—out of his cab and into the bracing Illinois cold.

Mike has his thick fist wrapped around a wooden billy club. He smacks each of the truck's tires to listen for the telltale sound of low air pressure. There are so many tires that you wouldn't know if one was going flat unless you thumped each of them. He has me try it so I can learn the sound of full inflation. While I'm doing that, Mike relieves himself in the gravel behind the trailer; I follow suit.

Back up in the truck, we take our seats, buckle in, and prepare to roll. We're now among the four million semitrucks on our nation's highways. Mike learned from dispatch that we'll start our journey close by, about fifty miles away in Waukegan, Illinois, where we'll pick up a load of gypsum pressed into drywall. That's always the goal, to minimize the time you drive with no load, what truckers call deadheading.

My first full day of long-haul learning begins.

"I run flatbed," Mike tells me. He confesses that he had to look up what that meant when he was told the kind of truck he'd be driving. He says he's hauled everything, including bulldozers— "That was pretty cool." He continues, "Some loads are easier than others. You throw a few straps, you're done. Other loads, you got to climb on top, use all your straps."

Other truckers consider their flatbed colleagues badasses. At least that's how flatbedders (or maybe just Mike) see themselves. That's because it's hands-on trucking with tarps, chains, and straps, and load configuration is mostly the responsibility and handiwork of the driver. It certainly isn't like hauling cases of Kleenex without lifting a finger to load or unload like those "dry-van people," as Mike calls them with a note of ridicule.

Mike's company runs all brand-new Volvos. Our ride is a 2021 Volvo VNL 760 pulling a fifty-three-foot flatbed trailer. Empty, we weigh 32,000 pounds. I take this all in, but with no coffee—Mike is not particularly interested in stopping for it—my brain is in low gear.

Mike points to his dashboard to show me his special trucker's GPS—he calls it his "main chick"—then he points out the standard GPS on his mounted iPhone 13, which he refers to as his "side chick." He explains the trucker GPS warns of the roads where truckers can't go. That sounds important. It displays upcoming truck stops and weigh stations as well as height and weight limits up ahead. Every good trucker always knows the truck's height and weight and is hypervigilant about overpasses and country roads. If they're not good truckers, they end up going viral on a YouTube video with their load wedged under a bridge.

Mike earns as much as three thousand dollars a week, which

makes him one of the top drivers at Ox and Eagle. In fact, it places Mike in the top tier of truckers in the country, since the median salary for all truckers is just over $47,000.

"They pay me top dollar. I double what some old-time truckers make at a company they've been with for their whole career."

The company started Mike—like all its new drivers—at a rate of 25 percent of the value of his loads. Other companies might start out drivers at varying rates per their experience levels, but at Mike's place, you have to prove yourself to the boss. Some companies pay drivers cents per mile, but the better deal is when a trucker earns a percentage of the company's gross for each load. Mike quickly jumped to a higher percentage and then to an even higher percentage. He proved himself.

Mike's best single-pay day was a triple load—meaning a pickup for three different customers—from JFK airport. That load maxed out his allowable weight at 80,000 pounds and put $2,000 in Mike's wallet.

After his near-death training torment in the Rockies, Mike won't drive the mountain states in winter. "I'm a Florida boy," he proclaims. Nevertheless, Mike certainly encounters snow in other locales. He always keeps a winter kit in the truck with extra water, packets of tuna, candles for warmth, and a lantern in case power to the truck is lost. He says he's prepared to be trapped for days on a blizzard-blocked or avalanche-addled highway.

Mike has traversed the cross-country routes to California multiple times. And he's made lots of trips to Illinois, Indiana, Michigan, Ohio, Kentucky, Tennessee, and Wisconsin. "You know," he said, "the manufacturing states that make stuff."

As we pull out of the lot, Mike lets me know that his electronic log starts registering as *driving* the second the truck exceeds five miles an hour. There are buttons to push for *on duty,* for *loading,* and for *off duty. Loading* could also be electronically entered as part of the mandatory thirty-minute break every eight hours. The log knows all and sees all—what you want it to know and, often, what you don't. You can hit the designation for *on duty—fuel,* or *on duty—pre-trip inspection* (we just did that), or *on duty—post-trip inspection.*

Mike says there's also "off-duty break for when I'm taking a shit or eating."

Hopefully not at the same time, I think.

His dispatch and his boss man can remotely track how fast Mike goes. The boss back in Chicago can remotely turn on the truck's camera and see what traffic Mike is battling. "One time I called the boss about bad traffic, and he replied, 'Yeah, I see that.'"

Mike says he knows truckers who have drones they fly out the window to scope out a traffic jam or check out an accident up ahead.

The logbook, or ELD (electronic log device), is in a perpetual electronic handshake with our truck. It knows the zip code we pass through. If Mike tries to extend his legal driving time by turning off the logbook and then turning it back on within the same zip code, it won't snitch on him. But if he turns the logbook off in one zip code and back on in another, an inspector or state trooper who stops and checks the log will know he tried to hide something.

At a big company—bigger than Mike's—hitting the rumble strip on the side of the highway alerts a company safety coordinator, who then calls the driver. Every night there's a legally mandated ten-hour "reset"—downtime—and every Saturday, Mike begins his required thirty-four hours off. That means no driving wherever Mike happens to be.

I figure with all this corporate tracking, there's far less of a chance that serial killers are company drivers. According to Truck Info.net, only about 9 percent of truckers are owner-operators—truckers who drive their own trucks and answer only to themselves. If my theory is correct, that shrinks the pool of FBI HSK suspects down to only about 350,000 truckers. Then again, maybe not.

There's at least one case where a trucker parked in a truck stop but rented a car to meet his victim. His truck stayed put while he beat and raped a trafficked woman. Renting a car was his regular practice, which facilitated his other practice: hunting for victims during his mandated downtime. There are also cases where the trucker picked up a victim during a quick stop, then committed his crimes along his route without significant delays. If those truckers were corporate, it might be easier to catch them based on their proximity to a dump site, but being company drivers certainly wouldn't rule them out as suspects. So much for my theory.

There are other safety features in Mike's semi. For instance, when he engages his turn signal, a horn blares inside the cab if there's someone in the next lane. It jolted the bejesus out of me the first time it happened. A good driver learns to instinctively scan all his many mirrors to maintain constant situational awareness and especially before he makes any moves. There are top and bottom mirrors on each side of the cab, and there are mirrors on the front hood corners. The big side mirror on top gives Mike a view to the rear of the trailer; the smaller bottom mirror displays the scene behind our cab.

"Look, this guy's not going to let me in—*ha*."

Mike is right—there's a car that won't yield to us.

"I *am* going to get in this lane. It's only a matter of time."

When he is finally able to maneuver all the way into the lane because another trucker lets him in, Mike flashes the exterior rear lights to thank him. It's a common practice that I see often.

Mike isn't dressed in what most people, like me or other truckers, think long-haulers are supposed to wear. Regardless of how cold it gets outside his cab, he's "a slipper-and-shorts guy, for comfort. I laugh at these guys driving box trucks [because they don't load or unload] but they wear the boots, the jeans, the button-down shirt: 'Look, I'm a truck driver.' When I pick up a load, of course, I'll quickly scan the yard. If everyone's in protective gear—safety vest and hard hat—then so am I. But otherwise, why be uncomfortable?"

Plus, Mike adds, "I sweat a lot when I'm strapping, chaining, and tarping a load."

(I confirm that claim later in our journey.)

Mike begins to explain his work rhythm and some of the rules that govern drive time. He drives for no more than eleven hours a day, works a total of fourteen hours six days a week, sometimes for two or three months at a stretch. "In reality you're really driving to your destination only about nine hours a day. The other hour you're often searching for a place to park for the night."

Which, I would come to learn, was easier said than done. If

Mike drives less than eleven hours, the log knows and doesn't require him to rest and sleep for the full ten hours. It gives him the time back to start driving earlier the next morning. The log giveth, and the log taketh away.

I note that these hours of driving mean a lot of sedentary time in the seat.

"Yeah, I gained too much weight last year—thirty-one pounds." He attributes that not so much to being inactive but to finally having money: "I wasn't used to having money—I was eating whatever I wanted. That's changed."

Indeed it has, because Mike and I already collaborated on a list of healthy groceries we'll pick up later so the CIA-trained chef turned trucker can cook some of our meals right in his rig.

I learn more about Mike BT—before trucking. He isn't hesitant to confide that he was a bad kid while growing up. There was fighting, stealing, bad grades, suspensions, and being booted out of class. "In middle school, I'd steal snacks out of stores just to sell them, make a buck. I'd break into cars—bring a backpack and steal all the change in everybody's consoles. Me and my friends would end up with fifty or sixty bucks' spending money. We'd have to hit a lot of cars to get that."

Mike began to shape up a bit in high school when he started wrestling. His brother was a very successful wrestler; he got Mike interested, and the coach recruited Mike because he needed someone in Mike's weight class. The coach was in his face a lot, which, Mike said, helped him "mature" and become more of a man.

"In my first tournament I went three and one. I had no idea what I was doing. But I would just grab them and throw them to the ground and pin them. Brute force and grit." This boosted Mike's confidence in a big way. "I wanted to beat the shit out of more people."

The discipline from his coach, which Mike said was often brutal and probably wouldn't be tolerated today, Mike loved. He thrived on it. It "put hair on my chest," Mike told me.

The story of Mike's coach prompts me to ask him about his father.

"My dad wanted two things—to provide for his family and to have a motorcycle that went really fast. My dad taught me to fight in the backyard. He told me, 'Don't ever throw the first punch. Don't let me hear that you were the first to lay hands on someone. But if they hit you first, you have my permission to beat the living shit out of them. In fact, if you do, I'll buy you a steak dinner. If you throw the first punch, you will be grounded.'"

While we talk, we roll past a disabled truck cab on the shoulder hooked up to a wrecker. Mike spontaneously mutters, as if telepathically communicating to a fellow driver he's never met, "Oh, I'm sorry, brother, I'm so sorry."

Mike feels this guy's pain. He explains that this trucker's breakdown translates to at least a day of downtime and maybe a load or two lost. "Definitely dollars down the drain." Hence Mike's empathy.

Mike owns a motorcycle. In any spare time back home, he works on his car-engine project. When he finishes that project, he plans to take his refurbished auto out on the racetrack, but he's quick to add he won't speed with it on the highway.

"I can't risk a ticket and getting fired by the boss man."

Mike clearly likes and respects his boss, Andrei, who owns

the company. Andrei is from Moldova, and his life has the hall-marks of a hardworking-immigrant success story.

Andrei had nothing when he came to America. According to Mike, Andrei drove a flatbed for about seven years, then found out he was going to be a father. He bought his own truck, which was cheap, and it broke down. Andrei bought a better used truck, then eventually bought a new truck, and he recruited drivers for those trucks.

Now Andrei owns five trucks, his brother owns two, and his cousin owns two, all under Andrei's company name. It's something Mike aspires to.

Interestingly, the dispatch team for Mike's company lives mostly in Ukraine and Eastern Europe. They sleep and wake in sync with American time. The lead dispatcher, Stefan, speaks English well, and Mike enjoys chatting with him during long drives. The first time Mike realized Stefan wasn't Chicago-based was when, during one of their many phone conversations, Mike offered to buy him a drink next time he passed through the city. "That would be nice," Stefan replied, "but I live in Romania."

Different immigrants and ethnicities are attracted to American trucking for a variety of reasons. Over the decades, old man Dale saw an increasingly diverse mix of ethnic groups in trucking—"Indians, Iranians, Middle Easterners," he told me. While over 72 percent of truckers are white and 12 percent are Black, it's easy to see why trucking increasingly attracts a kaleidoscope of cultures. The job offers decent income without demanding an American education or fluency in English. When people from a family or a village experience success, all their friends and relatives come to join them. Often, Dale observed, those ethnic groups, initially wary of the unfamiliar American culture, take a team approach to driving. They drive two or three at a time in the truck. Safety in numbers, perhaps; maybe sanity too.

Andrei pays his drivers more than other truck-company owners do. The good wages plus the trust Andrei builds with his team pay off in the form of respect. Mike describes Andrei as "a class act, a beautiful soul." He gives me an example of why he holds Andrei in such high esteem:

"I'd been on the road for two months and needed to go home to Florida. First, I had to drop off a load in Nashville, pick up my next load, then get the truck back to Chicago and fly home from there. When I get to my stop in Nashville, these people tell me, 'We weren't expecting you—we don't have a forklift here.' It was Friday; they couldn't unload me till Monday. The only way I'll get to Chicago in time for my flight is if I drop my load, get my next load, and drive back to Chicago. Andrei tells me he's willing to buy me a ticket from Nashville to go home. He said he would fly there himself, sleep in my truck, and unload it himself. He was about to book me on American Airlines. I told him no, stay home with your family. That impressed me."

Mike is chasing cash, and that means constantly cajoling the dispatchers on his phone headset to give him the highest-paying loads. Those are the tarped loads, the cargo that a client insists must be covered, as well as any bulky or awkward loads that have to be secured by heavy, thick chains. "Some guys just want an easy load but it won't pay well."

One of his most challenging loads—eight hot tubs in the pouring rain of Green Bay, Wisconsin—was difficult to secure because those supersize spas weren't designed to travel propped up on their sides like amoeba-shaped dominoes. It didn't help that they had taken on rainwater. He almost walked away from that load, but that wouldn't have been Mike.

Old man Dale certainly hauled plenty of odd-size loads. His most awkward was a sugar mill out of Houston. It was twenty feet wide. Dale recalled it and other such loads with a sense of pride.

"We did it at night. Had highway patrol escort us to Baton Rouge." He said he'd hauled airline wing spars—the skeletons of aircraft wings—out of Boeing in Seattle, to Oklahoma City, and to Wichita, Kansas. "I've hauled a lot of farm equipment too, John Deere and tractor combines. Big industrial air conditioners; I hauled some of those all the way from Detroit to Johns Hopkins University in Baltimore. They were twenty to thirty feet long and eight feet wide."

Flatbedders like Mike call unwieldy loads sketchy. "But sketchy really depends on the driver, how you choose to secure it. Probably the coolest load I've had was six Bobcats at one time. I had to lay ten chains. I'd rather lay tarps and straps than chains, but chained loads usually pay more, so fine with me."

There's also what truckers call suicide coils—densely heavy, gargantuan rolls of steel or aluminum that, if not properly secured, could break loose and barrel right through the back of the cab. Before our week is done, we'll haul one of those.

The law establishes the minimum number of required points of securement (I learned a new phrase) based on load weight and length, but Mike isn't a bare-minimum guy. "I'll over-secure a load with extra chains and straps."

Each one of the several thick braids of chains—pooled like pythons in the darkened den of a steel locker behind the cab—can secure ten thousand pounds. More commonly used are wide yellow winch straps, rolled up on winches that look like fat fishing reels anchored every few feet along each side of the trailer. They're good for five thousand pounds each.

"My maximum load for this trailer is forty-seven thousand pounds. I can handle forty-eight to fifty thousand, but I never want them to overload me. I also calculate the weight of remaining fuel in my tanks. Sometimes I'm so close on weight limit that I can't fully fuel up. There's also maximum weight per axle, so properly positioning the load is key. My company rule is that if I pick up a load of over forty thousand pounds, I stop at the nearest weigh station to verify it."

Who knew truckers had to be mathematicians?

There's another factor in how much a load pays—it's how fast the client needs it delivered. "Chicago to Houston is an eighteen-hour drive—that's not legal" for one driver to do alone. If the client wants it in the same day, a trucker has to have a partner who will take some of the drive while he's sleeping.

The same is true for a Friday load that must be delivered before closing time and ready for client use on Monday morning. A customer pays big bucks for that.

Today is Monday. Mike says that once we load what he calls our gypsum—which is actually drywall—we're going four hundred miles for a $1,900 load. He gets 30 percent of that. But he'd rather go six hundred miles for a better-paying load. "For me, it's about how much money am I making today? More is better."

As we talk about getting somewhere fast, I ask Mike how fast our rig can go.

"I can only go sixty-nine with cruise control, but if I use the gas pedal, I can get to seventy-one." A lot of the speed constraints for trucks have to do with fuel efficiency—which means they have to do with money.

"If I was allowed to go faster, I might squeeze in another load every week. But I'll burn more fuel. The company decided how they set the governor. Companies differ a little on this."

On the topic of money, Mike feels strongly that truckers don't know what they are worth. He says the big companies treat their drivers like they're expendable. "Just a number—if they quit, they quit." He names some names. "J. B. Hunt, C. R. England, and those guys—they pay half or less of what I'm paid. The governors on their gas pedals are set at sixty-seven miles per hour to save gas, which slows them down and leads to them making even less money. They'll say it's for safety, but it's more likely about saving money."

Mike tells the story of an old trucker at a truck stop he saw wearing a Schneider jacket. With about ninety years in the industry and nearly 20,000 employees, Schneider is a major player with a good reputation. The company hauls almost 20,000 loads a day in over 10,000 of its trucks. This trucker's jacket was covered in patches that denoted thirty-one years of service, plus he had safety-award patches—the guy looked like a highly decorated war veteran.

Mike couldn't resist asking him, politely, carefully, how he liked working there. The seasoned driver said that his company treated him all right. Eventually, Mike worked up the courage to ask his fellow road warrior how much he made per mile.

"Seventy-one cents," the man said proudly.

Young rookie Mike didn't have the heart to tell the old guy that he was paid by the load, not the mile, and averaged a dollar a mile at about 3,100 miles a week.

As the week progresses, I come to realize that compensation is more complex than Mike's initial description. He is single with no kids, and—to my chagrin—he thinks he doesn't need the health insurance that bigger firms provide. The big company guys are considered employees, so they get health care and other benefits for their families. Maybe the old guy in the jacket had put four kids through doctor and dentist visits and took paid vacation days with his family. Maybe that grizzled trucker didn't have to pay much at all for surgeries and MRIs.

The father in me wants to lecture Mike on the risk he's taking, but I hold off—for now.

Besides benefits, there might be another reason why certain truckers tolerate lower pay—they might be out of options. For example, Mike tells me that Western Express is considered a "second-chance" company—with a reputation for hiring a lot of ex-cons. He claims they aren't the only company that does this; in fact, Mike says, it's quite common in the industry. "A lot of felons. They'll hire you with a lot of speeding tickets too."

An app called Trucker Path shows truckers the way to truck stops like Flying J and Pilot (where Mike's company membership scores him free showers and points) and to Love's. The app even points to the best truck-friendly Walmarts, the ones with plenty of room for parking and that don't post the dreaded NO TRUCK PARKING signs. It even shares real-time intel from other truckers on how many spots are still open and has reviews of the food and showers at even the smallest mom-and-pop truck stops. Mike opines that there are too few truck stops for the number of truckers on the road. Before our week is out, I find myself in total agreement.

If you've ever seen trucks lined up along highways and off-ramps, here is Mike's take:

"Good luck finding a spot for the night after seven p.m. That's why you see trucks lined up all along highway on- and off-ramps. I got an eighty-dollar ticket for that during a check operation. That's a mark against me and the company. They have to create more places where we can shut down and sleep for the night. Sometimes I'll end up sleeping on a ramp at a rest stop. It's still not legit, but it's supposed to be a rest stop! We also have what we call a makeshift stop—somewhere on a truck-stop property that's not actual parking but it's also not blocking someone in. I sleep a lot better when I'm in a good spot."

When he's parked overnight at a rest area run by the state, the county, the feds, he says, "You're asking for an inspection and a ticket." That's because they literally own the place. At a private truck stop like Love's or Pilot, you're less likely to be inspected. In Mike's company, if a driver gets inspected and passes, the boss electronically sends him a hundred dollars on the spot. Mike said, "I've been inspected twice, and I got a hundred bucks on Apple Pay each time from the boss man. The company gets good points in the government's system for me passing, bad points for me failing."

Long-haul flatbed truckers move tons of gypsum, huge cable spools, iron, and steel. There are two even more respected badass-trucker types. First, the heavy-load guys—the drivers who haul over 80,000 pounds that you see carrying wind-turbine blades or giant generators, sometimes with lead and follow cars warning other drivers of a wide load or a heavy load. Then there are the lowboys—the ones whose trailers seem just inches off the ground because they haul outlandishly tall freight, like earthmovers or excavators.

There's another thing that sets flatbedders apart, and this is a point of pride for Mike.

"I can do a dry trucker's job with just a day of training to learn how to open and close the trailer door. But those guys would need a month and a half of training to learn all the particulars of securing different flatbed loads and the related DOT securement laws."

That means a flatbedder can get a dry trucker's job with ease, but not vice versa.

We arrive in Waukegan at one of the big gypsum plants to load 47,000 pounds of drywall. This place is "been there, done that" for Mike. As with this and each of our subsequent stops, when I'm not chatting with Mike, I spend some time on the internet learning something about our destination town, the company client, or the product we'll haul. It turns out that gypsum (calcium sulfate dihydrate), which is used to make drywall, is the connective tissue of the home-building industry. That means it's also a cash cow for the trucking industry. Truckers have nicknamed it "gypsy." As in, "I'm headed to pick up a load of gypsy."

Unless you live in a tent and work outdoors, chances are high that you're surrounded by drywall. The COVID pandemic slowed gypsum production and construction, so now home builders are screaming for gypsy. Mike and I have become a small part of a rekindled builders' supply chain. You're welcome.

It's still early, and I see only three trucks ahead of us. Two are already inside the giant loading doors. Outside, there's one other truck waiting. We pull up to start what will become a queue. Signs announce that hard hats and safety vests are mandatory, so we throw on our neon mesh attire, like we're flying colors for some garish street gang partial to orange and yellow.

Mike and I walk in through the human door next to the gaping garage portals. He shows his papers to some guy seated in the cramped office, whose unfazed response is "Yeah, go wait in your truck."

I try to take in the vastness of the operation through hazy white dust and the din of drywall being mixed, cooked, pressed, dried, and maneuvered onto waiting trailers by a small squad of workers wearing eye and ear protection and masks.

While we wait in the truck, more trucks join us. This is when I start to learn that patience is a prerequisite of the long-haul game. I ask Mike how long he thinks we'll be here.

"Well, almost everywhere we go, we'll be told the process takes an hour. If it goes over two or three hours, my company will increase its rate—it's called detention pay—and a small percentage of it will come to me, but not enough to make me whole for the downtime. I don't let the waiting get to me. It used to, but not anymore."

It's already gotten to me, and I just got here.

In about half an hour, the trucks ahead of us are loaded and it's our turn to pass through the towering bay doors, which stay mostly closed against the raw wind whipping off Lake Michigan, a couple hundred yards away. Mike pulls his rig out of our waiting spot, points the cab away from the garage, then angles the cab away from the trailer. He checks his mirrors, then slowly works the steering wheel until, somehow, we back straight into the loading bay; no easy task in this surprisingly small lot. I tell him I'm impressed and try to figure out how he did that.

Once inside, we dismount and watch as forklifts drop their towering stacks of drywall atop our flatbed until it literally groans under twenty-three tons of weight. I watch Mike as he stares at the forklift.

"See how he's bumping into the side of my trailer every time he drops a stack? That's going to leave marks on my trailer."

Mike doesn't want any trouble here. The forklift operator doesn't strike us as someone who is particularly jovial. Mike walks over and tries to talk with the forklift guy above the din of the factory noise. Mike gestures toward the trailer and motions his arms left and right, mostly left, toward the front of our trailer. Mike walks back to me, and I ask him what's up.

"I'm not thrilled with the position of this load. I like it a bit further forward on the trailer, just in case it's heavier than we think. But the guy promises it's not more than forty-seven K."

I make a mental note to ask Mike what this all means later, when we don't have to deal with the noise of the gypsy place. As it turns out, I learn precisely what it means, but it takes a while.

Loading takes maybe another half hour. Gypsy must be covered; even a brief bit of rain will ruin it. Mike keeps his thick, heavy black tarps rolled and strapped on the rear of his trailer. He frees them now so they can be unfurled by a worker suspended from a safety harness high up on our mammoth drywall mountain. Over the racket of factory and forklifts, Mike explains that this place hasn't always required the harness. He heard that someone fell off a stack like this and died. My eyes scan from the worker up top to the concrete floor below. It's a long way down.

For Mike, this is an easy load, because, as I will later experience, most of the time Mike is the guy who must climb up the load, secure it with clear plastic and then a tarp, then throw his winch straps to hold it all together.

Once the truck is loaded, we pull out of the bay and find a place behind the building where we can secure the tarps and tighten the straps down just like Mike wants them. We're just feet from the damp industrial shore of Lake Michigan. The sky darkens; the wind picks up; and seagulls take shelter under our truck. A solo raindrop finds my face.

"You feeling rain?" I ask Mike.

"Yep. Let's do this quickly," he replies.

With the speed and confidence of a seasoned pro, Mike raises aloft red plastic edge protectors that teeter on the end of a very long PVC stick, a system he devised to minimize having to climb on top of high loads. He places the protectors every few feet along the top edges of the stacks. The protectors sit over the protective tarp, but they'll be under the soon-to-come straps so that when we launch those straps up over the load and cinch them down tight, they won't dig in and damage the soft, impressionable drywall.

Last, Mike takes photos of the perfectly finished load and

sends them to the boss man. This way, if anything goes wrong with the load, we have proof of what it looked like at the start of the journey. Then he punches *driving* into the electronic log—as if it doesn't already know. With this much weight behind us, we will hit the first weigh station we see to ensure we are safe and accurate. We head for the open road.

"Look, I'm wide open on the pedal right now." Mike is letting me know just how heavy we are. Despite the fact that Mike has the gas pedal down to the floor, I feel barely any surge in power or speed; the speedometer says we are capped out at thirty miles per hour. It's about the load we're hauling. Mike seizes the teachable moment for me.

"That's all we have. People don't understand when they're cutting in and out around you on the highway how little power you have when you're loaded, how long it takes you to speed up and slow down. I can't get out of the way."

We're at a total weight of about 80,000 pounds and barely crawling as we hit a slight incline on the entrance ramp to 94 East. Mike puts his hazard flashers on as a warning to others, announcing, *We're coming, we're slow, we're heavy.*

Almost two hours south of Waukegan, we stop at a weigh station in Gary, Indiana. I know of Gary's reputation from my FBI days. Back then, the city had almost twice as much crime as the average U.S. city. Gary also lives up to its reputation when it comes to internet sites that advertise sex for sale. Anyone surfing those sites will find pages of local Gary ads and a handful targeting truckers.

You can't help but wonder if any of the women in those ads will be some trucker's next victim.

Mike and I pull onto the certified scales at the Pilot truck stop. In the old days, truckers used to have to go inside and get paper. Today, there's an app for that. Despite Gary's crime rate—which I hear has dropped—I'm not going to say that nothing good happens here; that wouldn't be fair. But I will say that nothing good happens to us. The weigh-in didn't go well. We are 1,000 pounds overweight. Mike calls his boss man.

This weight issue is more complex than I thought. Our problem isn't our gross weight. The "steers" axle under the cab of the truck can handle about 12,000 pounds. Back under the flatbed trailer, there's about ten feet between each axle. Those front and rear axles can each be loaded with 34,000 pounds. It's all about weight distribution. We are overweight on the rear trailer axle.

This happened during the load-up—of course it did. The drywall was placed too far back on the trailer, but Mike was assured the load was only 47,000 total, so how bad can it be? Maybe it is 47,000 pounds, maybe it isn't—but now it almost doesn't matter. Too much of our weight is on one axle. I can almost see the wheels spinning in Mike's head as he tries to troubleshoot this. His expression soon changes; he has an idea.

We try fueling up, right here at the truck stop, to increase the weight of the cab, which might take weight off the trailer. Once our tank is filled, we pull onto the scale again. But all that does is increase our gross weight.

One of the differences between a flatbed and a dry-van rig is that the flatbed's axles can't be adjusted. A dry van—the big box trailer—can slide its axles back and forth to redistribute weight. We can't do that, but we might be able to shift some weight if we adjust the connection between our load and the cab. So we decide to try moving what's called the fifth wheel, which sits under and between the trailer and the cab. It's a horseshoe-shaped plate on a pivot with a locking pin that connects the truck to the trailer. We try to slide that forward, but it's stuck, so we take turns slamming it with a mallet that Mike pulls from the truck. For the third time, we get on the scale. For the third time, we have a weight problem. It helped a little but not enough. Mike calls the boss man.

Consistent with Mike's description of the boss man as a stand-up guy, the boss decides not to risk the possibility of Mike's truck getting stopped while overweight. The boss doesn't want the ding against his company's record, and he doesn't want Mike to get a ticket. Dispatch calls the gypsum place that screwed up our load. Even though it's only two p.m., the loading crew has gone home for the day.

As is often the case in life, doing the right thing will hurt. We will again spend the night in the truck in Chicago so we can be in Waukegan bright and early tomorrow morning to have our load repositioned. This means Mike will likely haul one less load this week and not reach his target of a load per day.

But it also means there will be one less overweight truck moving across the states this week. How many other truckers and bosses do the right thing? How many overweight trucks are out there right now? Maybe one of them is that truck in front of or behind your own family's car.

Off we go, north on I-90 toward Chicago, an hour and a half away. Mike alerts me to something I have never paid any attention to, because I've never had to. It's a green highway sign that reads WEIGH STATION. Mike reacts. "Shit."

It hits me: If we get pulled into a mandatory weigh-in, we'll have a problem.

Here's how weigh-ins work. There's a device called a Pre-Pass in the cab above Mike's windshield. It looks a lot like an E-ZPass toll transponder. There's a little light on it. About a mile before the weigh station, an electronic reader identifies our truck, checks its safety and credential status, and decides if we should be weighed. All this happens in about a second. If Mike's PrePass light turns red, he has to pull into the weigh station. If it turns green, he can keep going. Mike told me there are times when he approaches an official weigh station and the light doesn't do anything. When that happens, Mike doesn't take chances; his practice is to pull in.

"Green," Mike says then.

Immediately, as if to confirm our good fortune, we see the weigh station and a sign that announces CLOSED; we both breathe a sigh of relief. Mike explains that even if we were found to be overweight, a ticket is not a certainty. He would have shown a trooper or inspector his app, which would prove that as soon as we weighed ourselves at the truck stop and realized that we had an issue, we headed back to where we'd picked up the load. Our story would likely allow us to avoid a ticket. Maybe.

But our luck doesn't last long.

An alarm goes off in the cab. It's brief but piercingly loud. I ask Mike what's happening. He glances down at his dash.

"The sensors on these new trucks are too sensitive. These alarms go off sometimes. Look, the warning light went on for engine coolant. It's probably nothing."

Sure enough, the warning light turns off, and the alarm doesn't come back on until, a few minutes later, it does—with a vengeance. It won't stop blaring. Mike checks Trucker Path for the nearest truck stop. Mercifully, there is a small stop up ahead.

Once we pull in and bail out of the truck, I spot a pool of amber liquid on the pavement under the engine. Liquid is cascading from the truck in an audible stream. Mike comes over to my side of the cab. If you've never opened the hood of a semitruck, it's not like popping the hood on your Honda Accord.

First, Mike pulls the release lever inside the truck at the bottom of the steering column, which releases the hood-latch locks behind each front wheel cover. Next, he folds the front grille guard down on its hinges, away from the grille. Last, he puts one foot up on the front bumper for leverage, braces his chest against the grille, and throws his arm over the top of the hood. Mike eases his body weight down, which causes the grille to go nose-down and raises the back of the hood skyward, exposing an angry engine awash in hot coolant fluid.

I spot it first. There's a fat hose that leads to the coolant reservoir. The hose has a small hole in it the size of a ballpoint-pen puncture. It's still spraying. Mike calls the boss man.

Lucky for us that we're in the Chicagoland area. The boss man is well connected here in his own backyard; he knows a guy. It's late in the day, but the boss man's contact promises to keep his shop open and wait for us. We run inside the truck-stop store, buy a bottle of coolant, refill our reservoir, and head for help.

The place looks more like a graveyard where trucks go to die than a hospital where rigs get revived. It smells even worse. The odor of raw sewage gags us. Like the boss man, this shop guy is Moldovan; he talks to us with a thick accent.

"I have bad news about this hose. It's the new kind of hose. I don't have in stock. I have to get from dealer."

Mike, ever the optimist, asks him: "Do you have any good news?"

The guy thinks for a moment and then, with an almost evil grin, says, "You can sleep here tonight."

The blank expressions on our faces must signal that we are not amused, because the Moldovan comes up with another idea. "You have the Gorilla Tape?"

"Huh?" Mike responds.

"You know, the Gorilla Tape," the guy repeats.

Mike and I forage through the cabinets on his truck, but he is all out of the kind of tape the shop guy needs. Yet when we reenter the shop, the guy smiles and holds up the hose like a proud angler who's just fished a two-foot-long walleye out of Lake Michigan. He found his own Gorilla Tape and wound it tightly around the hole in the hose.

"You are good," the guy assures us.

"We are good?" Mike asks.

"You are good," the shop man confirms.

We'll be good until the Gorilla Tape gives up the ghost, I think. The boss man, who mysteriously already knows what happened, calls Mike and tells him that this quick fix should put us back on the road to Waukegan and then to our delivery site in Ohio, and whenever Mike's route returns us to Chicago, we'll have a brand-new hose. I have my doubts about this, but I'm not the boss man.

Back in the truck, Mike assures me that the three things we experienced today—a weight issue, a stuck fifth wheel, and the coolant leak—are unprecedented. "Never happened. Never all in one day."

I tell him, genuinely, that it's good for me to learn about all these things, that this is why I want to ride along. But I'm wondering how long the tape on this hose will hold. It's getting late and dark, past the time most truckers have found a place to shut down for the night.

Our only option is the Gurnee truck stop, a small mom-and-pop place in rural Gurnee, Illinois. Real-time reporting from truckers indicates only three of the fifteen spots are occupied. The Trucker Path app gives rave reviews to Donny's Diner next door. We find a parking space and pull in. It's seven thirty p.m.—we're hungry and tired.

We walk into Donny's, but no one is there. Not a customer, not an employee. After we spend a few eerie minutes inside an unlocked business without a soul in sight, a woman enters the front door surrounded by the pungent waft of weed. She makes an announcement: "The grill is closed."

So much for that. Mike suggests we order delivery from Grubhub.

"Do you do that a lot?" I inquire.

"All the time," he says.

We place an order for Middle Eastern chicken and beef shawarma. We figure since it is protein and rice, it's a relatively healthy meal, as long as we skip the pita bread.

Since it's now Monday night, and neither of us has showered for thirty-six hours, we decide to use the truck-stop showers while we wait for our food delivery. The attendant behind the store counter is older, with longish unkempt hair, untrimmed fingernails, and flesh that is the kind of pale that comes from never seeing daylight. He has a pendant hanging from his neck and the creepy vibe of someone you wouldn't want near young children.

He tells us it will be ten bucks for a shower, and ten bucks more—refundable—for the key to get into the shower. Although the place has two showers, for some reason he only charges us for one. Mike clarifies something with the man. "You know we're not showering together."

The guy gives us a ghoulish grin.

"Where's the towels?" Mike asks.

Neither of us likes the response: "I only have two and they're dirty," says Dracula.

Mike has one towel in his truck. He offers me two of his clean undershirts to use as towels, and I accept. The shower feels good, as does brushing my teeth and changing my clothes. I'll come to appreciate these things more as the days progress.

It's places like this that recently convinced Mike to order an Isinwheel electric scooter. It offers Mike freedom for about four hundred bucks. When it arrives, he plans to store it in his truck, and when he needs to get to a Walmart or a restaurant or even explore a city on his down weekends, he'll park his rig and transition to two wheels. The boss man told him it will be no problem to keep the scooter in the truck. In fact, the boss man told Mike to ship it to the boss's house in Chicago and pick it up there. Mike figures he'll save a ton on Uber rides.

The Grubhub food arrives, and it's tasty and plentiful. I just want to go to bed after getting almost no sleep Sunday night. I'm never able to sleep right after dinner, but Mike can turn off like a light switch. He starts snoring as soon as his head hits the pillow. I catch about six hours, then wake up at three a.m., thinking it is much later. Nevertheless, I'm up. I slip quietly out of the cab and head into the 24/7 store.

There's a different guy behind the counter, less vampire, more ex-con. I pour myself a hot coffee so I can warm up. Despite the late April date, temperatures are still in the thirties. As I sip, I scan the shelves stocked with instant soup, ramen noodles, cereal, candy, nuts, beef jerky, and liquor. A refrigerated case holds sodas, energy drinks, and beer.

I watch as a male customer strolls in and goes through a door marked CASINO into a room attached to the store. Several minutes later, a woman, alone, enters the casino too. I head back to the rig, where Mike is still asleep.

Mike was a good choice to expose me to the real-time life on the road, but he is unaware of the long history of killings. If I want to learn the history of homicides on our highways and the coordinated pursuit of the offenders, only one person will do: the trailblazing Oklahoma criminal analyst Terri Turner.

CHAPTER 7

THE OKLAHOMA CRIME ANALYST

"It was a white female. She was nude, definitely a body dump," Terri told me of the September 2003 case that birthed the HSK Initiative. "There was this little pull-off from the road."

Renowned highway-killings crime analyst Terri Turner agreed to speak with me about her work for the Oklahoma State Bureau of Investigation (OSBI). "I've done a lot of interviews because the FBI can't or won't. That's okay."

She was right about my old agency. They declined to engage with me in a more protracted give-and-take discussion about individual HSK cases. The FBI was fine with preapproved scripted questions about the FBI database and available analytical help, but not much more. I understood where they came from. The HSK is all about supporting hundreds of cases belonging to other law enforcement agencies. The FBI can't speak for those agencies or pretend they know more about the investigations than those departments. That's where Terri came in. But Terri wasn't a second-best choice. She was an all-star.

When I spoke with her, Terri Turner was in her thirty-seventh year as an OSBI analyst. Before that, she'd spent five years working in communications with a local police department in Edmond, Oklahoma, a suburb of Oklahoma City. Terri was a supervisor and had been since 2009, and she oversaw the Crimes Information Unit (CIU), which provided analytical services to not only the OSBI but also other police agencies across the 70,000 square miles of the Sooner State and to district attorneys and the governor's office.

Terri's team used specialized software, open-source research, and law enforcement databases to identify bad guys, compile criminal histories, and provide invaluable insights to agents and detectives examining cell phone communications, establishing timelines, and creating graphics and court exhibits for successful prosecutions. Much like FBI analysts, Terri and her colleagues helped connect the dots that solved crimes across a city, a state, or even the country.

Terri was baptized in the murky waters of serial killings in September 2003. A local department called OSBI for help identifying a body found near I-40 in Tiger Mountain, Oklahoma. Densely wooded forests and undulating hills along Lake Eufaula offer some of the most scenic terrain in Oklahoma. The same feature that made Tiger Mountain a great place to hunt and fish also provided a nearly perfect setting to dump a corpse.

Back then, the woods of Tiger Mountain sometimes hid stolen cars and even meth labs. A couple of rest areas tucked behind lush greenery seemed to stir up their own crime waves. The secluded scene offered truckers a place to rendezvous with trafficked women who advertised their services on CB radio channels.

"It's known from California to Maine in the trucking business."

That's what former McIntosh County sheriff Bobby Gray told the *Oklahoman* in April 2001. "There's nothing good there to stop for. Good truckers aren't going to go there," Gray said.

Truer words have rarely been spoken.

At Tiger Mountain in September 2003, a trucker spotted the body of a nude white female. The woman's head and wrists were wrapped in tape. There was no ID.

Terri explained that her priority was identifying the victim. "Who is this?" is obviously a crucial question to ask when trying to solve a murder. Yet for an analyst, a close second is "Can we find any similar cases?" To help answer that question, Terri sent a teletype to a wide swath of the country's law enforcement agencies. It contained a general description of the victim and the crime scene and asked if anyone had had a similar missing person or a similar case. "In just two or three days, we learned of two similar cases."

There was one victim found near West Memphis, Arkansas, a small city across the Mississippi River from Tennessee. She was dumped off the on-ramp to I-40 westbound at mile marker 265 in Shearerville on July 11. That victim was in the sex trade and had last been seen at a truck stop in West Memphis.

The second case that Terri's teletype unearthed was from August. An unidentified body was found on August 20, 2003, under the Tallahatchie Bridge in the mudflats near Choctaw Ridge in Lafayette County, Mississippi. The whole scene sounded like a macabre remix of "Ode to Billie Joe," Bobbie Gentry's 1967 chart-topping single: "He said he saw a girl that looked a lot like you up on Choctaw Ridge / And she and Billie Joe was throwing somethin' off the Tallahatchie Bridge." Like the July and September victims, this woman had her head wrapped in tape. Terri now had three nude taped murder victims—"my girls," she called them. They were dying about every thirty days; it was as if the killer kept a calendar. Or maybe, like many serial killers—if that's who was doing this—his bloodlust couldn't be contained for more than a month.

How long has this been happening? Terri wondered. How long before it happens again?

There were no IDs found near any of the crime scenes. Eventually, the police put a name to the Mississippi body. She was twenty-four-year-old Jennifer Hyman, and she had recently been spotted at a truck stop in Oklahoma City. Jennifer, who was strangled, had been a college student trying to earn money to pay tuition. The West Memphis, Arkansas, victim was reunited with her name as well: Margaret Holmes Gardner, forty-seven. Terri knew what to do.

"So we started looking at truck stops; we started reaching out to police vice units."

That paid off. Terri's own Tiger Mountain, Oklahoma, victim was confirmed to be a "truck-stop girl" who had been working a stop off I-40 and Morgan Road in Oklahoma City. Now Terri knew that each of the victims was linked to commercial sex. "That gave us our victimology."

Terri contacted each of the police agencies who had victims and introduced herself. She took a cautious, nonthreatening approach to avoid any tensions over turf: "We have an unidentified—can we share information? Could you give me photos of your scene; can we coordinate and collaborate?"

No one turned her down. Some senior-level bureaucrats in Mississippi sounded reticent, wanting to keep their cards close to the vest, but rank-and-file detectives just wanted to solve cases. Those investigators assigned to what had seemed isolated homicides suddenly found that their cases were part of something bigger, more ominous—more urgent.

Once she had everyone's data, Terri approached her agency's leadership with the sobering reality: "We have three similar murders, in three states, a month apart—July, August, September. All but one victim was taken from Oklahoma. We should monitor all teletype traffic for anything remotely similar in other places."

Sure enough, before the calendar page turned, there was a fourth body. This one was right in Terri's backyard, north of I-40 in Oklahoma City. The next month, October, brought the fifth victim. A nude woman was dumped in the Texas Panhandle. It didn't take long to learn that she had been picked up in Sayre, Oklahoma, a small town halfway between Oklahoma City and Amarillo, Texas, alongside—you guessed it—I-40. A sixth body served as further confirmation that far from slowing down, this murderer, like many serial killers, was hooked on the rush of adrenaline streaming into his bloodstream, heightening his senses with every kill.

Like victim six, number seven was also found in Texas, this time outside of Grapevine. The calendar might have proclaimed a new year—it was January 31, 2004—but the story was eerily the same. Again, there was an Oklahoma connection. Casey Jo Pipestem was from Oklahoma City and was a member of the Seminole Nation. She had been raised by her grandma, but Casey was only seven when her grandmother passed. Casey was moved from the city to live with other relatives in remote towns, but the abrupt shift to rural living with alternating family members was like being dropped onto another planet.

In her teen years, Casey quit high school, returned to Oklahoma City, and slipped into the abyss of drug addiction. In a familiar tale, particularly for Native American women, Casey was exploited and trafficked for sex at truck stops in Texas and Oklahoma. Like so many trafficking victims, what Casey did to survive ultimately led to her demise. Beaten, raped, and strangled, nineteen-year-old Casey Jo was tossed off a bridge and into a creek bed.

As she learned of each new victim, Terri Turner made similar phone calls to what was now a growing list of police departments. She reached out to her local FBI field office too. Except for Margaret Gardner, all the victims had been taken from Oklahoma. And the body count was rising every month. Yet few people were really alarmed. "I wasn't getting much traction— even in my own agency. At times, I felt like I was essentially working solo."

Terri decided to do something about the "solo" part. She understood the essential need for everyone to be in one room to discuss and compare their cases. She reached out to the FBI's ViCAP and Behavioral Analysis Unit to ask them to come talk to everyone and see if they would help. Terri expected about twenty people from different agencies to show up: "It turned out we got sixty—it was standing room only. There were so many cases I didn't know about."

As might be expected when so many homicide investigators

from so many states and cities all showed up in one place, the media showed up too. Local reporters camped out waiting for somebody to say something. The OSBI public information officer had to feed the reporters a taste of what was happening just to make them go away.

The FBI agreed to open a serial case to support investigators, meaning that the Bureau's requirement to demonstrate at least three similar murders was met. After getting wind of that word *serial,* the media "went nuts," and so did the public, according to Terri.

"I was taking calls at my desk from people who said they knew a trucker or that they had another case for us to look at. I called ViCAP for help in managing this. Was there someone I can turn all this over to?"

The answer was yes. A young FBI analyst showed up and partnered with Terri for three straight days to make sense of the various streams of information flooding the files. Terri said, "It was an incredible partnership, and we got all the information coordinated."

Something happened after the press reported on the big investigative conference. Or, more accurately, something *stopped* happening—at least in Oklahoma. The bodies stopped piling up. That's not to say there weren't corpses dumped in other places; there were, and Terri's phone kept ringing. Had the killer been in Oklahoma and seen the local news coverage? Had he (serial killers are almost always male) decided there was too much heat to risk another body dump there? Terri kept wondering and working.

CHAPTER 8

CROSSING THE RUBICON

It would help pay for the heroin.

That rationale lured some of the girls next door—like Hannah, the Midwestern girl with broken boyfriends—past the point of no return. It was the most malignant milestone so far in their stumbling, struggling existence, a lasting before-and-after event that, regardless of where their paths took them, would forever mark the moment when a young woman traded a piece of her soul for cash or drugs. It wasn't only or always about being able to afford the next fix; it was more complicated than that. The affirmation and affection of older males, the pressure and influence exerted by exploiters, the desire to preserve a relationship that was just as addictive as a drug and that offered an illusory haven from trials and traumas—all ferried the soon-to-be victim across a river of hurt and into a world of pain.

Whatever the motivators were, the time inevitably arrived when sex was for sale.

For Nancy Yarbrough, the Wisconsin preacher's kid whose trauma started with inappropriate touching and worsened after her parents' divorce, it was the older influencers who pitched the idea of sex as a source of cash. "He was way older than me. And I just figured, why not? I'm already doing everything else. Let me see if I can find some creature comforts in all the hurt that I've experienced thus far. So, I'm like sixteen or seventeen . . . I'm thinking about, 'Hey, I'm already having sex, and I'm not getting paid for it.' And that's how he introduced it."

Nancy went on to say that she "started experiencing a different type of underbelly. The different type of world that is hidden in plain sight."

Hidden in plain sight like the truck stop we pass on the highway or the big rig that zooms by us on the interstate or the young woman standing in the back of the rest stop while we fuel up.

For other women, the predatory path was more incremental. The men in their lives started them off as strip-club dancers or placed them in the shadowy business of "erotic massage." In any case, those were entrance points to the peddling of flesh for someone else's profit. In these transitions, it was a simple case of more money for more services so they could get more drugs or more attention, affection, and affirmation.

There were no baby steps for Nancy Yarbrough. Pimps plunged her headfirst into trafficking at truck stops across I-94 in Wisconsin. It was her training ground for yet more marketplaces.

"We had to be groomed on what to watch for, in regard to the trucks . . . Learn the names and kinds of trucks. Learn the CB language. So that you don't end up getting arrested. How to vet the person that you're talking with to make sure they're not police officers. It was just a whole organized way of life."

Nancy was a small, light-skinned African American with blond hair. When she recently told her story to the public, she explained that even in the microcosm of Wisconsin truck-stop trafficking, there was racial segregation and economic disparity. White women worked one truck stop; Black women stuck to another one. Nancy's blond hair and mocha skin tone meant that she was permitted to work with the Caucasian girls. "We got paid more over there."

As was common practice for street-level and truck-stop trafficking victims, at the end of each night, the money Nancy earned went straight to her pimp. If she hadn't met the mandatory threshold of at least a thousand dollars, her night wasn't over, even if the rising sun claimed it was. She talked about the variables that determined how much she made for her pimp through transactions at truck stops and in other, much more varied environments.

"It just depends on the day. It depends on the county or the state that you are in. The younger you were, the more money you made." If you did parties and things like that, you could make anywhere from two thousand dollars to ten thousand dollars. "Depends on your clientele," she said. For Nancy, once she was trafficked beyond the truck stops, the clientele represented a cross section of society. "It can be anywhere between a Wall Street guy, the priest, the corner-store guy, the guy that drives the liquor truck. I had all kinds of buyers."

For Hannah, immersion in trafficking didn't start with truck stops. It was more subtle than that. She owed an employer some favors. He had been giving her advances on her salary, money she and her man kept blowing on dope. The boss had a client who was keen on Hannah. That's how it began.

It became nearly impossible to keep a roof over their heads.

Any available cash went to purchasing dope. Paying the bills was relegated to an annoying afterthought. Since Hannah and her boyfriend had no money for a security deposit and no legitimate employer to list on a rental application, apartments were out of the question. Cheap motels were the plentiful alternative. They charged by the week or month; there was no lease and no credit check required.

One young woman and her man, as they were burning through the girl's cash to remain constantly high, stayed at a well-known budget-chain motel for a whole year. She explained her view of these motels' business model: "Places like that trapped you. The fees were just high enough to prevent saving anything and just low enough to keep you from going somewhere else."

As addiction raged on, any money earned went to heroin; any heroin went in their veins. As tolerance to hard drugs developed, the two of them needed increasingly dangerous cocktails of illegal drugs. Practices like speedballing—mixing cocaine and heroin and injecting it in one shot—made money vanish quicker than the lovebirds could find a vein. Not even the threadbare weekly budget motel was affordable anymore.

The girl's inner turmoil and overwhelming anxiety, fueled by a combination of hard drug use, dangerous dealers, violent men, and weekly panic over whether the motel bill would get paid, were surpassed only by the traumatizing terror of selling herself to trucker after trucker, all night, every night.

Most victims, despite their misery, don't understand that they are being trafficked. They know only, often through a heroin haze, that they are being used. The anti-trafficking organization Polaris works to dispel myths about victims. One of those myths is that trafficking victims always want help to leave the trap that ensnares them. From the home page of the Polaris website, we learn that myth isn't reality:

"Every trafficking situation is unique and self-identification as a trafficking victim or survivor happens along a continuum. Fear, isolation, guilt, shame, misplaced loyalty and expert manipulation are among the many factors that may keep a person from seeking help or identifying as a victim. But the Polaris organization recognizes and rejects the myth that all trafficking victims are locked up or physically prevented from escaping.

"People in trafficking situations stay for reasons that are more complicated. Some lack the basic necessities to physically get out—such as transportation or a safe place to live. Some are afraid for their safety. Some have been so effectively manipulated that they do not identify at that point as being under the control of another person."

Shame was a roadblock too wide for these young women to bypass and ask for help. What would their family members think of them if they knew the truth? Drug addiction was bad enough, but telling your sister, brother, mom, or dad that the girl they loved was being sold to strangers—that was a bridge too far. That's one reason why contact with family members is often broken off. It's not that the victim doesn't want to speak with her loved ones; it's more that she can't bring herself to do it. Sometimes, it's the family members who decide they can't bear the pain of hearing about another failed rehab attempt or new arrest, who don't want to listen to the latest plea for bail money.

That's why sometimes the offer of help needs to be more of a confrontation. I heard several stories from these girls of elaborately staged interventions in which the victim suddenly found herself surrounded by caring friends and loved ones offering love and help. Too frequently, the girls' responses sounded like a script penned by an eternal pessimist:

"I have bills to pay."

"I'll only go if my boyfriend goes with me."

"I need time to think about this."

"How can I continue my life if I'm stuck in rehab?"

As if what the victim was going through was somehow "living."

Those excuses reflected a fear of the unknown. Yet there was another factor at play in the rejection of help: the fear of the known. Anyone who had been to rehab knew that detox, the first step in any rehabilitation, was the equivalent of sustained torture. The girls knew that the pain of detox was the only way to climb out of the hellfire of their misery, but the prospect of going through withdrawal again was enough to make the most despondent addict crawl the other way.

In fact, crawling, begging, defecating, and vomiting were all part of most addicts' withdrawal experiences, whether they were in plush private centers or waiting for hours in a big-city hospital ER. Usually, an IV sedative was administered—assuming a nurse could find a vein that hadn't collapsed from the brutal abuse of months or years of hypodermic heroin use. Next, addicts were transferred to a detox area for days of nothing but sleep, meds, and vital sign checks; they were usually unable or unwilling to eat a morsel of food.

If you survived the detox ordeal, you often got your first exposure to Alcoholics Anonymous or Narcotics Anonymous right there in the facility. They'd encourage you to keep attending meetings once you were out, and if you were fortunate, someone in AA or NA would offer to be your sponsor. You'd likely wait for weeks to get a space in a sober-living house—that is, if state funding or private donations were still in place that month. Then, unless you were wealthy and in a longer-term private setting, you were thrust out of the nest like a fledgling still missing some feathers.

There is good news and bad news about rehab success rates for addicts in America. A 2020 study by the Centers for Disease Control and Prevention and the National Institute on Drug Abuse concluded that about three out of four addicts eventually recovered. The bad news was the "eventually" part. Recovery seldom happened with the first attempt. In fact, victory took almost a decade of trying and failing and trying again. It was during the failing phases and relapses when a trafficking victim's daily struggle to survive looked a lot like a death march.

Repeated relapses inflicted unimaginable grief on a victim's family members. It was a figurative death by a thousand cuts, and eventually families slipped into their own survival mode to save themselves from the endless despair. Visits to jail or prison stopped, as did any form of financial rescue. The now desperate victim, bereft of money, hope, and friends, reached her most vulnerable point. She sank further into the quicksand of addiction and trafficking. At a time in her life when she most needed to be clearheaded, her brain was fried.

It was during those periods of despondency that Hannah

shoplifted, stole, ran scams—did whatever it took to pay for the breathtaking amounts of drugs the demons inside her demanded. The demons always got what they needed. As with so many other victims', Hannah's crimes led to prison. During one stint in a major American city, Hannah befriended an inmate named Amelia who had the bunk across from her. Amelia was white, younger—in her early twenties—and blond. And she had something Hannah didn't yet have: a release date. Aware that Hannah was newly single, Amelia offered to let her stay with her and her boyfriend when she got out.

Amelia was in jail for theft, or at least, that's what she told Hannah. Later—much later—Hannah learned Amelia lied. As Amelia was being released, she gave Hannah her number and was kind enough to put money in Hannah's phone account to accept calls from Amelia. When Hannah finally got out, Amelia and a guy named Keith picked her up and brought her to their house. There was another man there named Derek. It wasn't clear to Hannah where Derek fit into this picture. The one thing clear to Hannah was that these people had nice things; they had money.

Amelia was a drug user. In fact, all the housemates quickly shared drugs with Hannah. Inside her addiction-addled mind, Hannah thought: *How nice—but who does this?*

Who indeed.

This part of Hannah's experience aligned with those of many other trafficking victims. This was jailhouse recruitment. Only now does Hannah understand that Amelia was a bottom, the girl who oversaw the other girls. Hannah wasn't the only victim living in this hell. There was another house with more trafficked women. What happened next has a legal label: involuntary servitude.

In these cases, personal identification, cell phones, and belongings were taken by the captors. There was no way of communicating with the outside world, no means to travel somewhere else. Drugs were steadily supplied to maintain command and control of the newly acquired source of income. Beatings, rapes, and penetration with various objects reinforced the message that attempted escapes would prove deadly.

In this type of controlled operation, a victim might be trafficked through prearranged "dates"—at least one man a night—at clubs, truck stops, or motels for an average of eight to twelve months, or until she became more of a liability than a profit center. Among the clients were lawyers, family guys, cops. Some victims worked five nights a week, with two nights off. When I heard this from one victim I interviewed, I did the math: At twenty times a month for ten months, two hundred men had purchased the human being sitting across from me. It had been several years since her captivity, but I still saw the damage from a punch to her face. But even more, I sensed the trauma in her soul.

For Hannah, the dates around the big city continued until they were all blurred together by numbing trauma and narcotic-induced nod-offs that got her, semiconscious, through the torment of that night's date, and tomorrow's, and the next. Then came the truckers.

The first time, Hannah, Amelia, and two other girls were driven by Derek to a motel at a truck stop where the truckers rented rooms. Like Hannah's other dates, this had been prearranged.

Amelia ended up in a trucker's sleeper berth, while Hannah went into the motel. Word of Derek's girls spread among the truckers, so there were even more dates with more truckers at the very same spot. One time, Hannah was brought to meet a trucker off a highway near a well-known sightseeing destination. Derek's girls became an illicit attraction near a national tourist site frequented by busloads of families.

Hannah offered me a couple of trucker-related insights:

"The trucker dates are always shorter because the guys had to hit the road by a certain time. But those dates still paid about a thousand dollars."

"It seems like the truckers are either family men or single perverts."

Two extremes with no middle. There were the guys that Hannah called *creepy*, by which she meant "handsy, super-handsy." They seemed not to understand that this was a financial transaction, not a romantic interlude. Quite possibly, some of those men had never experienced the latter. Hannah saw more evidence of alcoholism than drug use among the truckers.

Trafficking victims' fears shifted into high gear with trucker dates. The fear was legitimate; anything could, and has, happened inside a truck. A self-contained crime scene on eighteen wheels required extra vigilance against the creepiest of clients.

CHAPTER 9

THE PIONEER PROFESSOR

Working girls who reject the services of a pimp are called renegades and outlaws. That was Dr. Williamson's explanation of the two nontraditional work styles found in street and truck-stop trafficking.

There were twenty-seven renegades in the research study. Williamson and Baker found that these women saw themselves as entrepreneurs, free agents, or independent contractors. *Renegades* was the term mostly used by pimp-controlled women to describe those who worked on their own. Sonya, who was pimp-controlled, explained this when she was interviewed during Williamson's study.

"There's a lot of girls out there called renegades," Sonya said. "A renegade is when you don't have a man . . . Some prostitutes are out there for a man, for a pimp. We're out there bustin' our ass to get our money for a man and, you know, these bitches are out here making money and going home and not giving it to nobody."

Some renegades had had trusted partnerships with pimps in the past but had been exploited. That's why they preferred working alone. Sometimes a renegade teamed up with a girlfriend to work the bars or the streets, but it was understood that each would earn and keep her own profits. Many of the interviewed women expressed a sense of independence and empowerment—women like Melissa:

"I don't have to ask for help to pay my bills and feed my children . . . I make my money for me. I'm not going to turn around and hand it to no man."

Renegades told the researchers they were motivated to work the streets to earn immediate income. Michelle credited the lure and addiction of fast money. She stated, "And I was hooked, I was hooked. 'Cause, you know, it was a good time . . . that's how I started."

The renegades in Williamson's research noted a dangerous downside to being out on their own: "I was always by myself. I never had anybody watch my back. That's probably why a lot of times, I got robbed and shit."

An increased risk of rape, robbery, and assault was part of working alone. When those traumas happened, the usual response was to self-medicate, hire the services of watchers, or carry weapons. After being repeatedly raped, Bree talked about always carrying a knife in her bra whereas Jody suppressed her experiences with alcohol and drugs.

Jody said she buried it in her subconscious. "I buried it with drugs and alcohol. I buried it. I buried it deep and I wasn't afraid to go out. I became a little more careful, a little bit. But the crack cocaine had taken over at that point, I guess it just stopped mattering."

It's tempting to lump renegades and outlaws together, since they both operate without a pimp; tempting, but wrong. Rene-gades are transactional—sex in exchange for money or drugs.

THE PIONEER PROFESSOR | 119

Outlaws, however, are in it for the hustle, as Dr. Williamson calls it.

Dr. Williamson studied fourteen women who were outlaws, or street hustlers. These women conned men with manipulation or force "for the purpose of swindling or robbing them of money or property." They would not live under a pimp's thumb and refused to comply with the basic premise of prostitution the way the renegades did. Instead, as Dr. Williamson explained, "in any encounter they expected to walk away with more than they'd agreed on. In fact, their entire approach was to manipulate, exploit, and even rob their tricks during a sexual transaction." Tammy, an outlaw, said it succinctly:

"You know, just different reasons why, you know, we call them tricks. Because you can trick them out of their money. That's when you don't really necessarily rob them, but you get the money before you do anything, and you take off. It's not robbing; to me it ain't robbing, because I'm not using any force to get their money."

Dale Weaver told me that in his years of experience, there were truck stops where the odds of guaranteed action applied equally to both having sex and being robbed, sometimes during the same encounter.

The Williamson and Baker study found that outlaws sometimes enlisted the help of a male or female partner in crime. An outlaw might have a boyfriend who was also a hustler. She wouldn't describe the boyfriend as her pimp, but often he arranged dates, provided security, or partnered in a scam to get money from a potential customer. Emotional and physical fidelity were important to relationships between an outlaw and her partner. Most women with this arrangement shared any money either partner brought in.

I wondered which category of work style might make a woman more likely to be a murder victim. Who were killer truckers more likely to kill?

A pimp-controlled sex worker is certainly prone to beatings, abuse, and addiction at the hands of her pimp, but as I came to learn, she also gains a degree of protection from the pimp, his bottom, and the wife-in-laws in the stable. Someone is almost always watching.

Renegades on their own are less likely to experience the kind of vigilance that comes with being under the constant control of a pimp. Yet without the relentless pressure to meet a quota, they have a greater say over when they work and where they work, and they can be more selective about their clients. And without a pimp, there might not be the dangers of forced drug addiction, addiction that impairs risk avoidance and judgment.

Then there are the outlaws—the hustlers. They earn their living ripping off their tricks. Obviously, they incur the wrath of their targets, who might violently retaliate. However, outlaws often have partners, and they strategize quick escape plans or threaten to blackmail their tricks. Not to mention the fact that few men are likely to call the police and confess that they've been robbed during a commercial sex transaction.

CHAPTER 10

TUESDAY WITH MIKE

It's dawn in Gurnee, Illinois. Mike does his pre-drive inspection; he walks around the truck, looks for signs of leaks, ensures all our lights work, and whacks each tire with his billy club. Even though he performed this ritual last night, he does it again now, and he explains why with stories of flat tires discovered by truckers in the morning from running over an errant spike or large nail and with hypotheticals about vandalism by a road-raging fellow traveler who thought Mike was the one who cut him off earlier. He punches *on duty* into the log, which ends our official ten hours of downtime, and we start our twenty-five-minute drive back to the gypsy facility.

While we drive, I do a search of the usual platforms where sex workers advertise, and it confirms that even in this relatively small village with a mom-and-pop truck stop, a trucker could have found some "commercial" here last night. One site boasts an ad from a blonde, maybe in her late forties, who claims she is in Gurnee. Other ads feature women who are likely Chicago-based and simply include Gurnee among the places they can travel, but this woman seems based in Gurnee. This ad says she is "trucker-friendly," and she can come to you (that's an outcall), or you can go to her (an in-call). I show the ads to Mike who, up until now, has been the one educating me. This is all new to him. Mike can certainly find his way around Tinder and other such apps, even on the road, but paying for sex? Not his thing.

We return with our gypsy load just as the place opens. Mike talks to the same guy in the same little office in the loading bay. Our dispatch called ahead and advised the business that they overloaded us on a rear axle and that we'd be back, but that doesn't make a dent in this guy's attitude. Mike asks if they are going to pull the tarps and straps off the load for him. They aren't. That's when we learn the plastic and tarp folks here are part of a totally different operation and company than the fork-lift team. We are supposed to drive around the building behind the loading bays and grovel before the tarp and plastic boss sitting in a white trailer.

Mike has people skills. He takes a calm, slow approach with the man in the trailer and explains we have already lost a day because this load put too much weight on our rear axle. Eventually, the tarp boss becomes sympathetic.

He makes us an offer: If we take the tarps and straps off ourselves, his guys will wrap the load again once it's repositioned. We accept the deal, but before we walk out of the trailer, Mike can't resist adding that we have to redo all the bungees on the original load because the guys placed them on backward, meaning the sharp ends on the bungee hooks are digging into our tarp, a sure way to poke holes. The man tells us his own tale of woe: He can't hold on to a tarp man for more than a week. It's a tough, dangerous job to teeter on top of the loads and avoid being crushed by forklifts, and it pays less than McDonald's.

It's sobering to hear that the folks who secure tons of cargo on the trailers traversing our nation's interstates can't cut it at a fast-food joint.

Mike and I remove the ship-sail-size tarps that cover our load, fold them like Brobdingnagian bedsheets, then roll them up and hoist them back onto the trailer. Our tarps are ten feet across the top of the load with an eight-foot drop on each side, so while truckers call them eight-foot tarps, they're really twenty-six feet across. Each tarp weighs about a hundred pounds. Mike tells me we are doing this in less than half the time it usually takes when he does it himself. Whether that's true or not, I feel useful.

We jump back in the rig and return to the queue of trucks to patiently wait for the mercy of the guy in the little office. Mike enters *off duty* into his log instead of *on duty—loading.* He doesn't want any more loading time eating into his maximum fourteen-hour workday or his seventy hours allowable for the workweek. Mike says he'd like to yell and scream at somebody here, maybe point out that this was their fault, but he knows better than that.

"I'm not eighteen anymore. Back then I might have hit somebody. I'm a full-grown adult now."

Through the week, my road partner frequently refers to the old days when he was young and more prone to pugilism for dispute resolution. Mike's wrestling prowess in high school seems to translate into a high confidence that he can take anyone, anywhere, if the situation demands, and back then, the demand might have been frequent. While Mike matured along the way and clearly has the verbal skills to de-escalate conflicts, he's had time to think about how he might handle the kind of trucker tempests he sees play out at truck stops. "I would never be the aggressor—never throw the first punch—but if something developed, I would lure the other guy in front of the truck where my dashcam could capture the other guy throwing the first punch."

The tall door to bay 2 rolls up and a truck emerges, fully loaded. Hopefully, we'll be next. We're motioned into the bay. Once again, this is easier said than done because of the remarkably small and tight lot. Mike executes another alley-dock maneuver, driving forward and then angling into reverse while slowly straightening the truck to back perfectly into the bay. He does it in one shot.

Mike explains to the forklift operator, the same one as yesterday, what needs to happen. The guy doesn't take this well.

"You want me to move your entire load forward off the trailer axle about two feet?"

"Yes."

Mike shows him his weigh-station app that indicated we were a thousand pounds too heavy over the trailer axle. The guy puts up a mild protest.

"That's how I always load it."

Mike feigns empathy, then tells him this still needs to happen. It takes their team about thirty minutes to reposition the thirteen pallets of drywall and then rewrap, first with new plastic and then with Mike's tarps. Not surprisingly, they do a lousy job of wrapping. I've been on the job a day and a half, and even I notice this.

But Mike stays silent until we safely pull out of the bay.

He maneuvers the rig back behind the building, does a walk-around inspection of the load, and shakes his head.

"I'm going to have to redo these bungees. Wanna see why?"

A hook that latches a bungee to the trailer bed has already worn a small hole in the tarp. That's because that bungee is secured with the open, sharp end of its hook up against the tarp. But then I see it—it isn't just the one bungee on backward, it's all of them. Every single one of about twenty bungees have their pointy hook end in contact with the tarp. We take them all off and turn them around. I have renewed respect for McDonald's hiring criteria.

I don't have to be reminded—in fact I wish I could forget—that we are still driving with a Gorilla-Taped coolant hose. Andrei calls Mike to ask how it's holding up and to offer his latest guidance.

"Let's replace the hose."

Andrei found a parts shop only five miles out of our way and called ahead for us. He tells us that they won't take his payment over the phone, so Mike needs to use his personal card and submit the cost with his expenses. No big deal. We pull into M and K Truck Center in Des Plaines, Illinois.

M and K is one of the biggest commercial truck dealers and supply centers in the Midwest. They have locations in Illinois, Indiana, Michigan, and Pennsylvania. Thankfully they specialize in Volvo trucks. The place is humming. Mike wants to use the bathroom, so until he returns, I stand in the line for customers picking up pre-ordered parts. Fifteen minutes later, we have our hefty new hose and are on our way. It isn't installed, mind you, but we possess it, which saves us the hassle of trying to find one if we get stuck in the middle of nowhere. That makes me feel better, since the middle of nowhere might be a frequent destination this week.

Back in the truck, I learn more about my trucker teacher. It's clear that Mike's passion and a large portion of his money goes to rebuilding his Lexus GS 300. It stays parked behind his friend's house in Florida while Mike works on it. He shows me photos of the project in progress the way I show photos of my grandkids to people. If there is a bell or whistle to be found for his GS 300—like aerodynamic side-view mirrors—Mike makes it his mission to find it. As we drive, Mike often dons his headset to work the phones in search of some elusive Japanese accessory.

East of Chicago we pass a lowboy truck hauling a backhoe.

"Look at that—that's a lowboy. That's the only badder ass than me on this road right now."

It's a reminder of the hierarchy among road warriors.

I guess Mike would think Dale Weaver is a badass. Back in the day, Dale was on the road for a month or more hauling strip-pit equipment for coal mining. When assembled, these mining machines weigh over a million pounds. They have a big container called a dragline bucket that's used to pull soil off the top of coal deposits. With the Wales company, Dale traveled to Kansas and transported these mammoth strip-mining machines at tortoise speed, averaging only thirty miles each trip. He pulled a couple of these trips every day. The ponderous pace with hulking, lofty loads demanded a lowboy to accommodate their combined height and weight.

You can think of a lowboy as an East LA lowrider on growth

hormones. Its trailer sits painfully close to the ground and gives the rig a funky vibe.

Dale also drove lowboys for three years with Daily Express out of Carlisle, Pennsylvania. Daily was a medium-size firm with over two hundred drivers. Dale said a lowboy truck could wear out in just two or three years—the strain on the engine was that high. The wheels would quit at forty thousand miles. But the money was good, about ten dollars a mile back then. Sometimes Dale needed a trailer with as many as thirteen axles to handle those heavy loads.

After almost a year and a half of hauling, it's still a challenge for young Mike to transition from driving a truck for months on end to driving his little GS 300 back home. He doesn't hesitate when I wonder about the distinctions.

"Absolutely. Like, it's completely different when backing up a car. If you want to back up toward the right with a car, you turn one way. If you want to back to the right with a flatbed truck, you turn the opposite way."

Mike doesn't miss a beat when I ask him to recount the first day on the job driving by himself. "It was Gary, Indiana. Most people would have quit."

When he survived his Rocky Mountain white-knuckle-whiteout-conditions training trauma, Mike spent a week at home in Florida. Rested, he flew back to Chicago to pick up his assigned truck and begin his first solo long-haul experience. As Mike's plane landed at O'Hare, he felt nauseated; in fact, he was fighting the urge to puke. When Mike finally got to the company lot and located his truck, the contents of his stomach, like his busted luggage, could no longer be contained. In the cold winter air, Mike threw up all over the lot. The retching rookie trucker was unsure what to do next.

"I think about calling Andrei and saying I can't pick this load up. But they had assigned my load two days in advance. This is my first drive without a trainer—and I'm a nervous wreck. I have to do this." Somehow, Mike managed to drive the truck to the load site. But his stomach wasn't done with him. "About fifteen minutes outside of Gary, I start dry-heaving out the window."

Andrei instructed Mike to call a time-out, get some medication, take a shower—do whatever Mike needed to do. But things got worse before they got better.

"I drive to the back of this truck-stop lot, and my truck gets stuck in ice. I start rocking the truck back and forth. I engage the button that locks up the rear drive axle to try and get traction. This doesn't work. It's eight or nine at night. I'm blocking the entrance to the back of the lot. I decide to call the guy who trained me. He tells me, 'Throw your chains under the tires'—but that doesn't work either."

Then Mike's luck took a turn. "I'm not religious, but somebody up there sent me this little chico." (Mike's term, not mine, for a Latino.)

The heaven-sent helper said, "Hey, bro, are you stuck? Want me to pull you out?"

The Good Samaritan tried chains and wood under Mike's tires. He was getting down and dirty under the truck, doing everything he could to get Mike out of the ice, including chipping the ice on the ground with a hammer. Then the mystery man hooked up a chain from the front end of Mike's tractor to his own rig and pulled Mike free from the frozen muck.

"I've been helping people stuck all night," the guy said.

Mike fell asleep for a while, woke up, and was still able to deliver the load on time. If you asked Mike, he'd tell you angels appear at truck stops.

Maybe, but so do demons.

One frosty evening near Moorhead, Minnesota, Timothy Jay Vafeades took the exit ramp to the Red River weigh station off I-94. It was November 2013, and the two state vehicle inspectors working that night had seen scores of compliant truckers come and go through their checkpoint. It was all routine, most truckers giving brief responses to the inspectors' queries. "But not Vafeades," one journalist wrote. "The man couldn't stop talking, as one of the inspectors, Cynthia Harms, would later recall in court testimony. Amid all the jabber, she couldn't help notice the tips of something sharp inside his mouth—something that looked like fangs."

The inspectors at the station processed over a thousand rigs a day. They got bad vibes when something wasn't right—and nothing seemed right with Vafeades or his young, silent, and bruised passenger. The inspectors ran the trucker's name and discovered something of interest: a 1999 Florida protective order. It gave the name of the young female whom Vafeades was supposed to stay away from—the same name Vafeades used to address his young passenger.

Vafeades's passenger turned out to be a relative he'd offered to let live with him in return for some clerical work at his trucking business. What he didn't tell her was that he would routinely sexually and physically assault her. Often beaten and choked to the point she passed out, the girl was effectively enslaved. Vafeades took all her forms of identification and her cell phone. Once Vafeades was in custody for the restraining-order violation, his victim found her voice. That's when detectives learned that for the past six months, Vafeades had raped and beaten the girl in the back of his truck. His victim was made to don fake vampire fangs, and her captor ground her teeth into points with a power tool.

There was more evidence of evil in the truck. Vafeades's computer and another hard drive were laden with child pornography.

As Eric Peterson detailed in his article "The Case of the Vampire Trucker" for Vice.com, media reports of the arrest produced another victim, referred to in court documents as Victim B, "who met Vafeades at a truck stop in Salt Lake City in 2012. She alleged Vafeades told her he would take her to dinner and instead held her hostage." For months, Victim B was physically and sexually assaulted by Vafeades. He made her cut and dye her hair, used a belt to whip her, and eventually forced her to marry him.

Police identified six victims of Vafeades, though the exact time and place of what happened to which victim is fogged by faulty memories and traumatizing terror. Many of his victims, including an eighteen- and a nineteen-year-old, recounted similar stories, right down to the fangs.

In November 2016, Timothy Jay Vafeades pleaded guilty to one count of transporting child pornography and two counts of transporting people across state lines for illegal sexual activity. In exchange for his guilty plea, other charges, like kidnapping, were dropped.

Compromises and deals are often a part of our criminal justice system. The weakness of insufficient evidence, wavering witnesses, and the distance of time are weighed against the strength of what police can successfully establish. Sometimes, that means certain charges slip away.

What confounded police in this case, though, weren't the charges that fell through the cracks but rather whether there were corpses deep within the dark crevices of those cracks. Was there some unknown victim that Vafeades had beaten to the point that she hadn't recovered? Had he choked a kidnapped captive until she couldn't be revived? If so, where were those bodies buried? No one knew, and Vafeades wasn't telling.

Mike and I finally make our Walmart run in Lafayette, Indiana. I don't know if Walmart's data analysts calculate how much the company earns from truckers, but from where I sit, in the passenger seat of this rig, Walmart and truckers seem hitched like a trailer to a tractor. On its website, the Trucker Path app actually markets itself in part as the best way for truckers to find the nearest Walmart:

"Easily find Walmart Stores nearby that allow truck parking. Trucker Path features over 3,500 truck friendly locations. With our free app you can always find overnight parking for your truck. Even read fellow truckers' reviews and check a location's ratings to make sure it's a safe place to spend the night."

For Mike, wasted time is lost money. That's why we strategized a plan to divide and conquer this Walmart. Since Mike and I want to eat healthy, we are mostly simpatico on what we will eat the rest of the week.

After Walmart, we make our way to I-65 south, then to I-465 due to construction in Indianapolis, then to I-70 toward Columbus to drop our gypsum. Mike facetiously remarks that he might as well buy a house in Indianapolis since he passes through there so often. Dispatch informs Mike that tomorrow—Wednesday—after we off-load, we'll pick up aluminum rods in Heath, Ohio, and haul them to Antigo, Wisconsin—160 miles northwest of Milwaukee.

This is the kind of load that pays well, in part because it comes with a strict deadline. We'll have to get from Ohio to Wisconsin by noon sharp on Thursday or the payment drops. The wheels in Mike's head start turning as fast as the wheels under the truck.

We'll need to off-load our drywall in Columbus early tomorrow, hope that the process goes quickly, drive deadhead thirty miles east to Heath, Ohio, load the aluminum, then hightail it to Antigo to make the deadline. This can help save Mike from being short a load this week because of the gypsum screwup. We'd wanted a shower and an overnight at a Pilot or Flying J, but those plans are out the window.

It's too late to get a spot at a truck stop. If you don't grab a place at a Pilot or Flying J by seven p.m., you aren't getting one. We try anyway, and indeed, every single spot is taken at 8:15 p.m. Mike calls dispatch and asks them to contact our Columbus destination for permission to park in their lot tonight so we can be first to unload in the morning.

Dispatch has no luck getting hold of anyone at our drop location, but Mike is determined to park the truck at their warehouse and sleep there. Off the highway, we make our way through dark city streets into an industrial warehouse zone. We pull up to the small lot in front of our destination. This is no warehouse. According to my quick internet query, it's more of an overflow storage building for a larger wholesale home-supply place in another part of the city.

More important, their back lot, which might be a safer place to spend the night, is surrounded by a barbed-wire fence.

There's a reason for the barbed wire. This is a rough part of Columbus. As if to welcome us, a staggering homeless man under the bridge repeatedly shouts at no one in particular. The whole area has seen better days. Yet Mike announces that this is where we'll spend the night. He won't risk a delay tomorrow. We lock our doors and take in the surroundings through our windows.

This place prompts Mike to bring up a topic that he's raised before. Maybe he sees it as a teachable moment for me. Mike says places like this make him wish he could travel with a firearm. I am sympathetic; I spent twenty-five years with a gun on my hip. But each of the various states he transits has its own rules on who, where, when, or if you can be armed within its borders.

Dale Weaver carried a gun. Back then, most states considered a gun inside a rig to be "stored" and therefore legal. The exceptions were places like New York and Connecticut—you know, "Those places," as Dale called them with an air of disdain.

"The Canadians confiscated my forty-four Magnum when I hauled a load of farm tractors up there on my way to Quebec. The customs officers saw my copy of *Gun World* or some other monthly firearms magazine and figured I must have a weapon. 'You have to have one—where is it?' they asked me. They searched my truck and found it. I lost my gun and got hit with a four-hundred-fifty-dollar fine."

I asked Dale what percentage of truckers back then carried guns. He said it wasn't something the guys talked about. Then again, Dale wasn't much of a talker.

My conversation with Mike naturally rolls into why we have fifty different gun laws in fifty different states, and wouldn't it make a lot more sense for Congress to pass just one federal gun law for the whole nation? I don't bother to remind Mike that I'm writing a book about truckers who kill, sometimes by shooting their victims. Those killers don't seem to care much about the myriad gun laws in various states. It's getting late now, too late to solve America's gun and violence issues. It's time for me to ascend to the top bunk and try to sleep.

CHAPTER 11

THE OKLAHOMA CRIME ANALYST

The autumn of 2003 brought falling temperatures and climbing body counts. Terri Turner watched the number of victims rise from seven to eight, then nine, then ten, scattered like autumn leaves finding their final resting places across Oklahoma, Texas, Arkansas, and Mississippi, then in Pennsylvania, Indiana, and Tennessee.

Word got out that the police suspected a long-haul trucker. Terri and her FBI ViCAP colleague partnered with Grapevine, Texas, police detective Larry Hallmark, who was on the Casey Jo Pipestem case. They forged a tight team, traveling across the nation to share what they knew in meetings and conferences, sometimes two or three a day. Like energized evangelists converting the lost, they preached their gory gospel to anyone who would listen.

The team visited trucking companies, law enforcement agencies, and—most important—the pool of potential victims.

"Larry would talk to girls working the truck stops," Terri told me. "We're not vice, we're not narcs," he assured them. "We're here to tell you that someone is out here trying to hurt you."

The approach worked. "That got us another case. A victim who was choked—she could barely talk, but she called Larry."

That victim, a fifty-one-year-old truck cleaner from Okla-homa City, told Larry she'd gone to a man's truck on September 12, 2004, to discuss payment for cleaning the wheels on his rig. When she got in, the trucker locked the doors, beat her, raped her, and choked her. She passed out and woke up on the side of I-35 near the Kansas border.

Investigators got to work as the victim reported what her attacker told her: "I just broke your neck."

The woman repeated something else the trucker said—something that got everyone's attention: "The first three, four, I killed, it bothered me, but I kind of like it now."

Detectives searched a trash can near where the victim was dropped. In this case, a killer's trash turned out to be the cops' treasure. Amid the garbage was a bloodstained bag from a hamburger joint. It was stuffed with trucking logs from a company with a driver whose signature appeared to be *Carl W. L.* Two days later, police searched a Lincoln, Nebraska, apartment and found several items stained with blood. Carl Wayne Lawson was arrested in Lincoln on September 21, 2004, just nine days after the attack. His nearly strangled victim picked him out of a lineup. Lawson's fiancée, Shauna Parker, spoke her mind to reporters.

"He's probably the biggest teddy bear and he's always respectful of women, saying yes ma'am and no ma'am . . . he's not a violent person."

Apparently, Shauna didn't bother to check that with Carl. If she had, she might have learned that Lawson told police he and his truck-cleaning victim had smoked crack together and gotten into a loud dispute at the truck stop when he accused her of stealing his cash. Lawson said he hit her, cut her, locked her in a storage bin under his sleeper berth, and let her out about seventy miles later. Just a big teddy bear.

Lawson immediately became "a person of interest" in the ten other homicides. Police took a DNA sample from Lawson to try and match it with the evidence in other cases. There was palpable excitement within homicide units in cities and counties across the country. Could this be the guy? Was this nightmare over?

If Carl Wayne Lawson was the key to answering those questions, his DNA wasn't opening any doors. There was no laboratory match. In 2006, Lawson was sentenced to eleven years in prison for what he'd done to the truck-cleaning lady.

Back home in Oklahoma, Terri teamed with a vice detective who understood that this wasn't about arresting women for solicitation; this was about saving their lives.

"He did the talking to the girls. He'd tell them, 'We need to know about someone who spooks you—someone who triggers your ick factor.'"

It turned out Terri had made the right call when she partnered with the vice cops. Vice held the key—or, rather, the ink—to identifying a lot of previously unidentified victims. That's because vice units routinely photographed the tattoos of the women they arrested or questioned.

Tattoos signaled membership in a particular gang or proudly proclaimed rank, like *Bottom Bitch* in a stable of girls. Some even advertised the name or literally the brand of the pimp who trafficked the flesh the ink adorned. Those photo files, which included a girl's street name, proved invaluable when matched against tattoos of deceased victims who were photographed— for the last time—by a homicide detective.

Detectives weren't Terri's only partners. The trucking companies joined the team. That made for a monumental task for Terri because there are over 813,000 private carriers in the United States. Terri developed relationships across the spectrum of long-haul enterprises:

"From the little bitty companies right up through the Werners and J. B. Hunts. I call and tell them, 'We may have a problem with one of your drivers, and I'll need some records.'"

Terri wasn't making small requests. Sometimes she needed to know every truck that passed through a particular truck stop at a specified time. Then she'd ask for the files on certain drivers.

"That meant the companies had to pull gas tickets, shower receipts, and Qualcomm records—the data from onboard computer software containing GPS navigation, electronic logs and messages. No one said, 'You need a subpoena or a search warrant.' They just wanted to help." Even back then, trucking companies conducted some semblance of background checks on drivers. They called around to other companies, checked some references. But Terri knew the holes in that process: "If a trucker bounced around enough, you'd miss something."

And that's when a trucker wasn't trying to be evasive. If he had a reason to try—for instance, if he was killing women—a trucker could make pulling his records nearly futile.

"We could analyze reported movements all day long, but if someone is running off their route, which was more possible at that point in time, the data wasn't very helpful. Was the Qualcomm turned off? Was it not working?"

These weren't hypotheticals. Terri spoke from experience—experience with truckers who didn't want to be tracked. Truckers like, as Terri and Larry later learned, the monster named John Williams.

Detective Larry Hallmark never gave up on finding Casey Jo Pipestem's killer. If it wasn't Carl Lawson, then it was somebody else who needed to be taken off the nation's highways and put in prison to live out his remaining days. At least nineteen suspects were identified and actively pursued by the investigative team. Hallmark interviewed trucker after trucker who remembered seeing Casey. Almost all of them said, "She was a sweet girl and did not deserve to die."

Casey hadn't trafficked herself. She had been pimp-controlled. Larry and the other investigators, including FBI agents, were adamant about at least finding and convicting whoever turned Casey into commercial property. They made it their mission.

The guy who'd trafficked Casey had sold other girls too. He pimped an adult woman, a sixteen-year-old girl, and a thirteen-year-old girl. He might still be at it if Larry Hallmark hadn't caught up with him. Detectives interviewed the man who claimed he was Casey's boyfriend and realized he was transporting girls from Oklahoma City to Amarillo, Texas, and trafficking them along the way. According to the charges, one of those victims was Casey's younger cousin. On March 5, 2005, a federal judge in Oklahoma City sentenced twenty-five-year-old Kelvin Scott Jr. to ten years in prison for child sex trafficking.

Detective Hallmark testified at Scott's trial. So did some of Scott's victims, including an underage girl whose age required the courtroom to be closed. An FBI agent who testified in the case told the court that Scott's thirteen-year-old victim was "addicted to methamphetamine and had mental-health problems, including self-mutilation."

Convicting Casey's pimp was only partial justice for Larry Hallmark and his colleagues. They became attached to the girl they would never meet. The *Fort Worth Star-Telegram* talked to Larry about the case he simply wouldn't quit.

"As much as all the investigators had done on these cases, I just knew that one day we would get a break."

On June 4, 2005, the popular television series *America's Most Wanted* featured Casey's murder. After the episode aired, a chilling call came into the show's tip line.

"My nephew made a comment about killing a pretty little Indian girl," a woman named Norma revealed. Her nephew was former trucker John Williams, soon to be known as the "Big Rig Killer."

Norma ended up talking to Larry. Aunt Norma had just visited Williams in prison in Mississippi, where he was doing time, along with his girlfriend, Rachel Cumberland, for the murder of a woman they'd met in a casino there. After she and John discarded the remains, Rachel worried that someone had spotted them at the casino with their victim, and she flipped out. In what must have seemed like a good idea at the time, Rachel called the police with a concocted story about finding a body. Rachel's story didn't hold up under scrutiny by detectives.

Quickly, the FBI's BAU helped Larry prepare for what could be the most consequential interview of his career.

"If you would show Williams a picture he would identify the victim."

The problem was that none of the photos of Casey that Larry displayed to Williams rang a bell. Larry decided to ask Casey's family for pictures in which Casey wore clothing she might have had on while working truck stops. They did. It was those photos that triggered something in Williams's murderous mind. Larry explained it.

"Williams snapped his fingers and said, 'That is Little Bit. I killed her.'"

Larry knew that Casey had had *Little Bit* tattooed on her shoulder.

On the road, Williams came up with his own routes outside his assigned deliveries, and he regularly offered to quietly take another trucker's route, maybe when that trucker was sick or wanted some time off. There was no need to tell the management. Who would know the difference? As long as the load got delivered on schedule.

Over time, Williams proceeded to rattle off the terrible details of the case. According to Detective Hallmark those details "included admitting to strangling Casey from behind." The psychopath also included this particularly maddening morsel: Williams left his truck to go shower and eat while Casey's corpse was still there. Williams, already suspected in the murders of fourteen other women and eventually confessing to thirty, was charged in Casey's death too. Even with a confession, a case had to be built, and evidence had to confirm everything spewing from the mis-wired brain of a serial killer.

Williams also confessed to killing Buffie Rae Brawley, a twenty-seven-year-old trafficking victim from Toledo, Ohio,

Dr. Celia Williamson's hometown, whose body was discovered in Indiana. Buffie was choked and her face was wrapped with duct tape. That's where Terri Turner's vision of an established network of investigators working similar cases paid off again.

Indiana cops interviewed Williams, and they eventually obtained his confession to Buffie's murder because Larry Hallmark from the Lone Star State introduced himself to Captain Clarke Fine from the Hoosier State at a conference in Reno, a conference just like the one in Oklahoma City. In Reno, Hallmark and Fine had commiserated about their unsolved cases. After Williams confessed to killing Casey Pipestem, Hallmark picked up the phone and called Captain Fine.

As with Casey, Buffie was pimp-controlled. Buffie had been trafficked along the highways when she was just thirteen. In his Mississippi prison cell, John Williams told Captain Fine all the details he knew about Buffie, including the tattoo of her daughter's name on her leg. Williams admitted that he had sex with some victims postmortem. He let Fine know that Buffie's head was lacerated because he'd hit her with what he called his tire thumper, what Mike and I used to strike our tires and listen for the lower-octave sound of low air pressure.

"The second she tapped on my window, she was a dead woman," Williams told detectives.

Yet confessions aren't convictions, especially when a suspect retracts everything he said. Which is precisely what John Williams did.

For now, police considered Williams a suspect in the violent deaths of:

Samantha Patrick (9/2002, Oklahoma)

Margaret Gardner (7/11/2003, Arkansas)

Jennifer Hyman (8/20/2003, Oklahoma)

Sandra Beard (9/18/2003, Oklahoma)

Vicki Anderson (10/16/2003, Texas)

Sandra Richardson (11/22/2003, Mississippi)

Patsy Leonard (1/1/2004, Oklahoma)

Casey Jo Pipestem (1/31/2004, Texas)

Buffie Rae Brawley (3/24/2004, Indiana)

Nikki Hill (7/18/2004, Mississippi)

It was nearly a decade before John Williams was prosecuted, convicted, and sentenced to life in prison for killing Casey Jo Pipestem. He and his girlfriend Rachel were also charged with killing Jennifer Hyman, the young lady found under the Tallahatchie Bridge, but that charge was eventually dismissed for lack of evidence. And while Rachel would be sentenced to twenty years in the Mississippi Correctional Facility for the murder of the woman from the casino, she was released after only eight years.

The life sentence meant that Williams might never kill a woman again, but that sentence didn't answer any questions. How many more women had John Williams murdered? Were all the killings he confessed to really his own?

If the answers were out there, no one knew where to find them.

CHAPTER 12

PROGRAMMED CODE

It turned out that Derek had an extraditable warrant halfway across the country. That's how Hannah escaped her captors. Derek and his girls were on a shoplifting spree at the mall. Security called the police; they ran Derek's name, found the out-of-state warrant, and carted him off in cuffs. It's also why Hannah got charged with retail theft and sent right back to jail.

Exchanging captivity for incarceration wasn't unusual for trafficking victims. It was not only an escape but a chance to detox before entering the jail's general population. Sometimes, jail was the only way that the fog started to lift. A clearer head and some time to think allowed a victim to contemplate questions about her future, like where to go when her sentence was up.

For many, like Hannah, this meant finding an AA sponsor, attending meetings, and complying with special drug-court parole conditions, like urine testing and group therapy.

Addicts had to distance themselves from places and people who were part of the problem. Frequently, that meant a new peer group centered on AA or NA and group therapy sessions. After all, those folks had a lot in common. There was a lot of fellowship among their circle of friends in recovery; they spoke each other's language, shared each other's pain, knew each other's stories. It's no surprise, then, that sometimes those recovering addicts fell in love with each other.

For a traumatized recovering woman, a boyfriend committed to getting sober was better than a man intent on getting high or exploiting her for profit. A date with a guy from the group might have been the first time a victim went out with a man whose only objective was dinner and a movie.

A love interest to share the journey to sobriety made all the difference for many in recovery. As months passed, life looked good—better than good. But sometimes, while one partner publicly progressed, the other silently relapsed. Sometimes drugs came back in the house and were way too close for comfort. It was all part of the eerily similar stories of drug-addicted trafficking victims who tried repeatedly to get it right even as everything went wrong again. Wash, rinse, repeat.

A relapsed partner could pull the rug out from under a victim's recovery, but so could other things. For instance, a medical procedure that resulted in a well-meaning nurse or doctor administering the one dose of painkiller that sent a former girl next door back into addiction, back to the darkness of selling herself for a fix. One victim I spoke with said the mere mention of the word *heroin* could trigger a craving that led to catastrophe.

It was no surprise to hear that trafficking victims got pregnant. Some had abortions. Yet occasionally a victim in a romantic entanglement with the baby's father would decide to have the baby, perhaps as a symbol of hope or a source of unconditional love and affirmation. The question of who would care for a baby, born into seemingly endless cycles of addiction and sex trade, drove the parents of a victim I interviewed to obtain legal custody of their grandchild. The young lady told me she understood what her parents did, but those legal papers served on her were like a cold, hard slap of reality. The reality that she was not the mother she needed or wanted to be.

It was in the despondency of yet another relapse that many victims returned to trafficking; it was as if they were following a programmed code. This was also where the seemingly well-defined categories of work styles—pimp-controlled, renegade, outlaw, as taught to me by Dr. Williamson—started to blur and shape-shift, just like the professor said they might. Previously pimp-controlled women, having learned a thing or two, became renegades. Women who were renegades might then backslide into a different way of working under someone's control, often for drug dealers who were fronting them dope in return for "working off their debt." That was a debt they could never pay back—not as long as they needed their drugs.

Trafficked veterans might launch straight into outlaw status, targeting men with rip-offs and hustles. One desperate trafficking victim who had been pimp-controlled told me that after repeated relapses, she marketed herself and even other women in exchange for drugs and cash.

Although it seemed to defy the imagination, a return to the trafficking life was almost always darker, more dangerous, and more deadly than the victim's earlier experiences. The hard drug use was all-consuming, the capacity for rational thought had vaporized, and the odds of being beaten and raped within the sealed confines of a truck cab or left for dead near a highway truck stop skyrocketed.

The odds also climbed for committing more crimes, like reselling shoplifted merchandise while they were high and needed cash for the next high. It was likely that a woman who was caught for those other acts would be carrying dope or paraphernalia on her. This was how past and present crimes stacked on top of each other on a rap sheet that now included drug charges.

Hannah couldn't escape those odds. She was eventually sent off to the state penitentiary. It was inevitable.

Dr. Williamson's words echoed as I listened to one victim. At the time, this young woman didn't know the terminology, but she had transitioned from pimp-controlled to renegade after suffering extreme exploitation. And while many renegades worked in tandem with other women for the sake of security, this woman partnered with a male friend, another addict who also sold his body.

Professor Williamson's lessons on drug-impaired judgment applied here too. This victim had plunged headfirst into the high-risk deep end of a cold, pitch-black pool. One frozen, desolate night, badly beaten by a trucker, she decided to end it all. Her male friend found her hanging from a rope around her neck. He saved her, and the rope scars eventually faded, but the suicide decision remained.

It was in this similarly dark chasm where Hannah, for the third time in her life, was for sale at truck stops.

If only there were people who could intervene, women who could warn Hannah off, tell her their own horror stories, take her in and lift her up. Such women existed. The ones I discovered were hundreds of miles and several years separated from Hannah and her plight. Yet they had things in common with her—addiction, trauma, and, eventually for Hannah, even more.

CHAPTER 13

A STARFISH IN THE DESERT

I'm early, but I decide to ring the doorbell anyway.

Two young ladies, probably in their twenties, open the locked door and greet me with smiles. One of them holds a toddler—a boy—in her arms. Upon hearing that I have an appointment to meet Dr. Dominique Roe-Sepowitz, they light up as if I've announced the imminent arrival of a rock star.

"Dr. Sepowitz is coming?"

"She is," I confirm.

I've just parked in the small visitors' lot steps from the front door of Starfish Place in Phoenix, Arizona. It's a community dedicated to the healing and empowerment of human-trafficking survivors and run by Dr. Sepowitz, associate professor and director of the Office of Sex Trafficking Intervention Research at Arizona State University. If Celia Williamson is the elder sage of social work and trafficking, Professor Sepowitz represents the new generation who have built on Dr. Williamson's work. The two women, in entirely different regions of the country, immensely respect each other. In fact, Dr. Williamson recommended that I speak to Sepowitz, and Dr. Sepowitz is thrilled that I already consulted with Williamson.

The young women offer me a seat and some water. I sneak

a peek into the nearby computer room/library, where a third young lady works at a computer. The ladies tell me that this woman is the mother of the toddler they're caring for now.

"She's working on a job application," they proclaim with pride.

There is no single solution to transitioning a trafficked victim from survivor to thriver. One size never fits all. And the harsh reality of funding and resources always plays a supersize role in shaping what solutions look like. Dr. Williamson's wrap-around model places the victims at the center of a wide variety of offerings of essential community services while those victims remain in the larger community. There's also another, more costly model that puts the victims and the services under one roof in the form of a centralized and subsidized residential environment. That model makes a lot of sense to me, yet it is increasingly rare because it's so cash- and resource-dependent.

I want to experience this kind of environment firsthand, hence my trip to Phoenix to visit Starfish Place and learn of its impressive impact.

On cue, Dr. Sepowitz makes her entrance, complete with an entourage of a couple of graduate-student assistants. Sepowitz is in perpetual motion, a blue-eyed blonde bursting with almost more information than I can process while walking and talking. First stop is her office—tiny and crammed with donated toys, diapers, and other items, and somewhere, under stacks of files, her desk. "This is what a social worker's office looks like—when they even have one."

The good doctor leads me down a hall and into a large open room with rows of tall round stools at high rectangular tables.

As we take our seats, I spot flyers on each table announcing an upcoming self-defense class for women. Dr. Sepowitz tells me there are also acupuncture clinics, cooking classes, parenting sessions, and a host of other services delivered to the women here.

There are also starfish. Starfish jewelry for sale to raise funds. Starfish artwork on the colorful walls. Before I learn about how this place works, I want to know how it got its name, so I ask. It turns out the name is from an old parable that I vaguely remember from somewhere.

The original tale is usually attributed to Loren Eiseley in a volume called *The Unexpected Universe,* published in 1969. In 2006, the story was adapted into a children's book called *Sara and the Starfish.* In one version, an old man spots a young child on a beach littered with starfish. The child is tossing the creatures back into the water. The old man addresses the child.

"There's too many. You can't save all their lives—it doesn't really matter."

The child throws another starfish into the water and says, "It matters to this one."

To practitioners like Dr. Sepowitz and Dr. Williamson, their staff, and countless others who strive to rescue trafficking victims, each life matters.

Dr. Sepowitz was in prison early in her career, not as an inmate but as a social worker. That's where she learned that 60 percent of the women behind bars were trafficked. And that's what prompted the professor to start a therapy group for victims of abuse and trauma and continue that work for six years at a place called Dignity House. After that, she ran a city sex-work-diversion program in a women's jail. She has trained more than thirty graduate students to run that therapy group. Dr. Sepowitz also taught dozens of her colleagues how to build and maintain similar programs. Learn it, do it, teach it.

Anti-trafficking social work initiatives are understaffed, overworked, and poorly funded, and anyone who runs them must learn to be creative. Dr. Sepowitz is no exception. Social work professionals agree that locking up sex-trafficking victims doesn't work and doesn't make sense. Yet the trafficked are still repeatedly thrown in jail. Once jailed, a victim calls her pimp, who posts her bond, gets her released, and becomes her hero. As the cycle repeats itself, the pimp's stature increases, and the victim becomes less likely to trust the police enough to tell them that she wants out. That's why experts like Dr. Williamson and Dr. Sepowitz constantly search for what they call alternatives to arrest.

But, as Dr. Sepowitz explains, simply not arresting them is not enough. Not being arrested means the victim stays on the streets or at the truck stops—unless there's somewhere else to go. It's a two-part challenge: enable the police to do something other than arrest and provide the victims with an off-ramp that leads away from trafficking. But how?

In her earliest efforts, Dr. Sepowitz created a collaboration with the cops. She eventually found the right officers with the best problem-solving mindsets in the strongest decision-making roles. The police understood the futility of the revolving door of prostitution arrests. They saw the same girls over and over, all spiraling downward into drug addiction and physical abuse. Those law enforcers were ready to get creative.

What the community came up with after seemingly endless hours of research, discussion, and throwing ideas against the wall to see what stuck was an agreement that applied an already existing tool in a completely different way to help sex-trafficked children. Arizona law allowed police to place a twenty-four-hour psychiatric hold on individuals who were a danger to themselves or others, and that included people with apparent drug or mental-health issues. Well, underage-sex-trafficking victims almost always had identifiable drug problems, mental-health problems, or both, and they were almost always in danger. When such a hold was placed, the State of Arizona essentially became the victim's guardian. That temporarily removed the child victim from the criminal justice system and avoided an arrest. But then what? The twenty-four-hour clock kept ticking.

As for meeting the challenge of quickly reaching adult victims identified by the police, Dr. Sepowitz and her law enforcement friends partnered with approved agencies and organizations throughout the city who agreed, on a space- and resource-available basis, to offer the kinds of services that might actually help victims change their situations. If it was drug addiction, the partners would find a treatment center able to support a victim that very night. If it was mental health, similar calls were made until some agency or facility could accept the victim. It didn't always work, but it was a start.

On top of the startlingly high percentage of trafficking victims among incarcerated women, Dr. Sepowitz learned that many of those victims had been trafficked before they were eighteen. In 2011, Sepowitz met a Phoenix police lieutenant who told her his own simple truth: "It's usually too late for us to help when someone is already trafficked."

He spoke of a joint FBI and Department of Homeland Security cross-country trafficking project aimed at intervening in the process as early as possible. The professor and the policeman talked about decision points in a young lady's life and finding a way to identify the advertisements for commercial sex that were most likely to involve underage victims.

Like Dr. Williamson, Professor Sepowitz lives in two seemingly disparate worlds: academia and real-life street-level solutions. But those environs are mutually dependent. The university setting demands data and research on what happens in the real world, and clinical solutions require tangible data and research to attract grant money and deep-pocket donations.

Dr. Sepowitz's heart was passionate about underage trafficking, and now she had to wrap her hands and her head around the cold, hard facts of the darkest corners of an elusive underworld.

Dr. Sepowitz decided that if pimps used advertisements to find men interested in juvenile girls, so could she. Sepowitz figured placing the same kind of ads would allow her to study the demand side of the economic equation. There had already been research on the girls, but what of the men who purchased them? Sepowitz hypothesized that measuring demand might help quantify the size and scope of the problem. Even more, perhaps exposing the men might shed light on how to lower demand. She devised a strategy that involved placing fake ads using language that implied the girl for sale was way too young. Plan in hand, the professor approached her police and community partners and solicited funding.

Swanee Grace Hunt—former U.S. ambassador to Austria—helped finance the placement of ads on the notorious Backpage .com classified listings in eleven cities. The ambassador also funded phone lines and other necessities. Then the police and community groups crafted a plan to conduct interventions.

Dr. Sepowitz and her colleagues tracked the calls from men in response to the ads. The men received a message: "You called a number today that could belong to a trafficking victim."

In some cities, an undercover cop called the man back and gathered more facts or set up a sting. In other places, a task-force officer called the man and identified himself as law enforcement to spook the guy so he wouldn't do it again. For some men, the exchange may have been the wake-up call they needed. But for others, not so much. A handful of men simply moved on to other ads and made the same calls, only to find themselves talking to the same detectives.

Ultimately, Professor Sepowitz became an expert on how online ads worked and how to flag adult- and child-sex-trafficking victims. Backpage was the number two online classified-ad service in the United States, after Craigslist, and the "internet's leading forum for prostitution ads," according to the U.S. Justice Department. A U.S. Senate report found that the service had manually and automatically removed words that indicated the person being advertised was a child, terms like *little girl* and *Amber Alert*. Backpage would then post the cleaned-up ad. In 2018, the DOJ seized Backpage.com and charged seven people in a ninety-three-count federal indictment related to facilitating interstate prostitution and money laundering.

Dr. Sepowitz's ad work drew the attention of some big-name Hollywood stars. In 2014, actors Ashton Kutcher and Demi Moore cofounded Thorn to counter child sex trafficking. Thorn engineered new technologies to combat online child sex exploitation in what it called a digital defense of children. Sepowitz's team became one of Thorn's more than seventy nonprofit partners in over twenty-one states working to use technology to protect vulnerable kids. (In September 2023, Kutcher relinquished his role at Thorn after he received heavy criticism for writing a letter to a presiding judge in support of a fellow actor convicted of rape.)

The fake ads were just one part of an overall study of underage trafficking in the participating cities. Detectives and analysts in those cities shared the specifics of their market. The collected data gave greater insight into the who, where, when, and how of the illicit marketplaces. Was it primarily an online problem? Was it linked to nightclubs and bars? The street? Hotels?

The approach and its results helped forge a more effective, data-driven policing playbook. The strategy also earned Sepowitz's team a role in the Super Bowl.

In 2014, with help from Cindy McCain, wife of the late Arizona senator John McCain, Dr. Sepowitz conducted the first Super Bowl–trafficking study. Cindy McCain publicly brought attention to what had become almost a tradition of trafficking around the Super Bowl and its related festivities. High-wealth individuals and celebrities, the kind who could afford Super

Bowl tickets, often wanted to see and be seen at the big game. But some of those same folks did things they wanted kept in the dark.

The McCain Institute provided funding to study the Super Bowl problem at that year's game in the Meadowlands in New Jersey. The entire New York metro area served as the arena for Sepowitz's study. Fake ads were placed in each of the five boroughs of New York City and in northern New Jersey.

Unfortunately, not everyone was playing on the same team. In Sepowitz's rookie Super Bowl appearance, a police officer assigned to the task force decided to call his own plays. Instead of following the plan to identify underage victims and assess the demand for them in this market, he arrested one hundred women who were authentic ad placers. He treated likely trafficking victims as criminals. Whatever that officer's misguided motivation, the arrests made a splash that might have spooked some men who would have otherwise responded to Sepowitz's ads.

Despite the unplanned arrests, plenty of men responded to the bogus ads for young girls. The Super Bowl experience also allowed researchers to study real ads by identifying the most common signs of trafficking and underage victims. They created a matrix checklist, later adopted by police in nine cities, to help prioritize and focus limited resources where they were most needed.

The project identified ads suspected of trafficking underage victims. They found hundreds of real-life underage victims. News of the success quickly spread. A Phoenix police officer headed a central Arizona project based on the study. The Las Vegas police department executed a strategic shift in their approach to prostitution because of the study results.

Even the U.S. Department of Defense came calling.

The Defense Advanced Research Projects Agency, or DARPA, is home to scary-smart people. The tiny agency within the DOD researches and develops innovative technologies for war-fighting and national security. DARPA recruits as program managers the leading scientists and academics in their respective fields and rotates them in and out every three to five years. That approach keeps ideas fresh and relevant while minimizing the crippling inertia found in many bureaucracies.

The big brains at DARPA decided to pay a visit to Dr. Sepowitz in Phoenix.

DARPA's interest in the ad project seemed a bit odd to her at first but their angle soon came into sharper focus. The feds sought a smarter, faster way to sort through oceans of information across the internet to find the nuggets of interest to the military and intelligence communities. The result was Project Memex, a twenty-million-dollar program that applied newly designed artificial-intelligence tools to the task of finding the proverbial needle in the haystack.

Since the underground human-trafficking business heavily relied on a significant web presence to attract customers, it offered an ideal proving ground, plus the added benefit of helping humanity. DARPA went to thirteen cities and taught law enforcement and human services groups how to apply artificial intelligence to find signs of trafficking across online ads and postings. It certainly didn't hurt that DARPA bought existing ad research data from the Sepowitz team for $135,000.

It didn't take long for Project Memex to pay off. Search engines programmed to scour the internet, including the dark web, for online behavior signals helped detect trafficking across the thirteen cities. A phrase like *new in town* hinted that the woman might be trafficked from one place to another. *Fresh* often meant the person was underage. The program also noted when different ads contained the same phone numbers repeatedly used by organizations selling multiple women or when branding tattoos appeared in photos of women. All these clues and many more generated leads for investigators who no longer had to hunt through millions of ads to find the ones linked to trafficking.

There were hundreds of arrests and convictions across the United States as the program spread to thirty-three police agencies. Eventually it was used by twenty-six cities in the United Kingdom. The U.S. Department of Defense, typically focused on waging war abroad, had joined the battle against human trafficking and saved lives in the process.

Throughout all their various initiatives, Dr. Sepowitz and her team never stopped searching for arrest alternatives. The police in Phoenix and the sheriff's office in Maricopa County became critical partners in efforts to make fewer arrests and refer more trafficking victims to places where they could get the kind of help they required. In the city of Phoenix, 80 percent of those arrested for prostitution over the previous ten years had been trafficked. The police didn't need to be told that they had a problem. They just needed help with solutions. Out of those partnerships, Project Rose was conceived.

The team found a church willing to allow its property to be used for a diversion program. On Thursday and Friday from noon to midnight, three police vice squads brought in girls, women, boys, and trans people whom they otherwise could have arrested for prostitution. The police delivered a different kind of message: *You're not under arrest, but there are folks who want to offer you some help.*

The project quickly diverted over one hundred victims away from trafficking and into much needed services. At the centrally located church, social workers, prosecutors, and the police repeated the refrain that they were not there to make arrests, they were there to make a difference. Detectives debriefed victims on whether they had seen specific suspected killers or rapists. Some said, "Yes, I've seen him."

Project Rose was a success, but it wasn't without controversy. Some people claimed that the police forced them to come into the diversion center. Others didn't like the fact that the location was a church and alleged that religion was being thrust on them; it wasn't, Sepowitz says. There were also claims from adult sex workers that Sepowitz was conflating forced trafficking with all sex work and treating everyone like a victim.

Dr. Sepowitz tells me the assertions were false. Sometimes when you are making a difference in people's lives, you make enemies too.

After five years of Project Rose, the city of Phoenix approached the professor with an offer she couldn't refuse.

The city officials had a new apartment building that had lost its funding from the U.S. Department of Housing and Urban Development. The residents had moved in about nine months prior but now they all had to leave. The city asked Dr. Sepowitz if she had enough victims to fill the building.

Starfish Place was born.

Opened in 2017 for trafficked mothers and their children, Starfish Place is a joint project of the city and Arizona State University. With a maximum capacity of fifteen residents and their kids, the place is almost always full. HUD provides residents who are unemployed with a voucher to cover 100 percent of rent; employed residents get a voucher to cover 30 percent. A grant from Cindy McCain helps provide in-house clinical services. During my visit, the corridors and courtyard were filled with energy, promise, and smiles.

"Come on, let me show you around."

Dr. Sepowitz brings me to a pantry filled with food items for the women and a log for them to record what they take. There are classrooms and meeting rooms. The place is bright, clean, and spacious. A woman is singing an aria from an opera, powerfully, in one of the rooms.

"That's an ASU music student volunteer. She uses the music room sometimes to practice when she isn't teaching music to the women or their children—they love her."

Sure enough, a few little ones outside in the courtyard, maybe six or seven years old, hear the singing and come running up to the locked glass door as if summoned by the Pied Piper. It's time for music class. Sepowitz opens the door, and the kids excitedly try to squeeze their way past her. Sepowitz reminds them of the rules: "First you have to ask your mothers."

They stop. One kid turns and shouts to a young woman pushing a stroller across the yard, "Can we go to music?"

"Yes," the woman responds.

The other kids run off to find their moms and seek permission.

We walk outside, where I see a one-story U-shaped configuration of attached one- and two-bedroom apartments, their doors all facing the manicured grass of the courtyard and the concrete walkways. As we start our stroll, moms pair up and walk, and even more young kids play tag or hide-and-seek. The children are clearly comfortable with Dr. Sepowitz and not at all shy about approaching me and asking who I am and if I want to play. I ask their names and ages; they ask me mine. One boy reminds me of something I already know:

"You're old."

The moms are just as curious but a bit more subtle about who this guy with Dr. Sepowitz is. In my peripheral vision, I catch one young lady flashing a quizzical look and a furrowed brow at Dr. Sepowitz. The professor reassures her: "This is Frank—he's a friend of mine."

As we continue down a walkway, I notice another woman looking at the professor and silently mouthing a question: *Who's that?*

"It's just a friend," Dr. Sepowitz tells her.

It doesn't take me long to process what's happening. Men are scarce around here, and rightly so. Sometimes pimps or drug dealers turn up and try to talk to their former "employees." Hence the reason why all the doors remain locked. Most of the men in the women's past exploited them, including some of the cops they'd encountered along the way. And there is always the possibility that any cop visiting this place might be investigating something or someone from the women's past.

About 22 percent of the women at Starfish Place are trafficked before their eighteenth birthday. "There's a high prevalence of intergenerational trafficking," Dr. Sepowitz tells me. "Thirty percent of the women have a relative—their mom, grandma, sister, or aunt—involved in trafficking."

Not surprisingly, a lot of these survivors successfully complete drug rehab. One woman who passed through Starfish has been clean for sixteen years. There are also victims involved in what the professor called "forced criminality." One woman robbed banks for her trafficker. Others were made to serve as drug couriers, ferrying meth across the border.

There's another glaring statistic that Dr. Sepowitz turned into action. One out of every three or four trafficking victims has been in a special-ed program in school. That means there is an identifiable group of school-age kids that can benefit from early intervention. In partnership with the Center for Exceptional Children, Dr. Sepowitz developed prevention programs. Now special-education teachers receive training and have access to educational materials and a school-based website.

This is all part of a continuous effort to answer two questions: "Who is most at risk?" and "What can we do about it?"

Prison inmates are another of the identified at-risk populations. The bottoms in pimps' stables refer the girls they meet in prison straight to their pimps. The pimps put money in these girls' prison accounts before they even get out. It's all part of a spotting-and-assessing recruitment operation. So the Sepowitz team stepped up to offer training within corrections programs. And when Arizona provides prisoners with electronic tablets, those devices are monitored for signs of trafficking recruitment.

Project Rose remains. It's evolved to place even more emphasis on arrest alternatives. The venue for the diversion shifted from the church to a senior citizens center and it occurs every six months. In neighborhoods with trafficking issues, flyers announce TODAY IS THE DAY and WHAT DO YOU NEED TODAY? Federal grant money provides free meals at the center, where there's a medical clinic, STI testing, mental-health services, and programs offering drug and alcohol detox—all on that day.

Sometimes, the diversion program goes street side. There's a hotel outreach with Phoenix police officers who respond to real ads for sex. Hotel rooms are set up in advance for when the seller shows up for a date. That's when a female undercover tells them, "We're not arresting you."

If the woman or man has a felony warrant or is selling drugs, that can be a different story. But if not, they are taken right next door to rooms where Dr. Sepowitz and others are waiting. There is testing for HIV, information on domestic violence shelters, and a wide variety of other services. Survivors speak to the women and tell them there is hope. The follow-up data on connecting people to the services they need continues to be impressive. Even the police praise the program as helping to increase trust among law enforcement and this hard-to-reach group.

CHAPTER 14

WEDNESDAY WITH MIKE

Nature calls at five a.m. I slip down quietly from my bunk, try-ing not to wake Mike, step to the front of the cab, and use my now-empty gallon water jug. While I'm at it, I note a car parked in front of us with a woman passed out in an awkward position in the back seat. I figure she didn't start her day yesterday in-tending to sleep in a car in a high-crime area, but life must have thrown her a curveball. I'm suddenly grateful for my bunk, as spartan as it is. I climb back up top with Mike still snoring.

Mike's alarm chirps at six a.m. I heard him using his jug and getting dressed. I stay up top so as not to magnify our "too many people, too little space" reality. When I finally drop down, I realize that there's also a young teen boy asleep in the front passenger seat of the white car still parked in front of us. That must be his mom lying across the back.

Maybe they chose this place to park because they saw our rig here and figured it was safer than their other options.

Mike enters *on duty—pre-trip inspection* into the electronic log. We're eager to drop our drywall here and move on, but there's no sign of anyone at the old brick building. We try the doors but find them locked. Mike and I walk around back, alongside the barbed-wire perimeter fence, and try those gates—no luck.

I search the internet for the company's phone number and read it aloud to Mike. He calls and speaks to someone who confirms we are at an overflow storage location, and we can't see a forklift operator until eleven a.m. Mike asks him if we can drop the load at their main location. I can hear the unfortunate response.

"No, there's no room here."

When we are back in the truck and out of the 35-degree chill, Mike contacts his dispatch and explains that the day hasn't started well for us. We still need to drive thirty miles east to Heath, Ohio, pick up our aluminum, and drop it in Wisconsin by noon tomorrow. Mike's Wisconsin payday is evaporating. Dispatch tells Mike to try to coax that guy on the phone into giving us an earlier off-load, but we already know the eleven a.m. forklift sounds firm. The dispatcher hints that maybe he might have a word with the guy, perhaps make it worth his while to get a forklift operator to show up sooner. Mike informs me that this wouldn't be the first time for such a negotiation.

With the prospect of some downtime, we start fantasizing about having a real breakfast in a real sit-down restaurant. Mike speaks longingly of a possible omelet in his future. I dare to dream of hot coffee. But like an illusory oasis to desert nomads, our vision dissolves when someone climbs up and knocks on Mike's window.

I think it's either a cop or we're getting robbed. Thankfully it's the forklift operator arriving hours early. Mike rolls down his window.

"Are you my lifesaver?"

He was indeed. Mike and I pop outside, quickly remove the tarps, straps, and bungees, and prepare for off-loading. We back the rig down an alley and pull up alongside a gate in the chain-link fence. Half an hour later, paperwork signed, we are on our way from Columbus to nearby Heath, where 42,000 pounds of aluminum awaits us—theoretically.

When we pull up to the security gate of a sprawling manu-facturing campus that belongs to one of the biggest aluminum fabricators in North America, a large sign instructs truckers to stop and call the posted phone number. Mike calls. I see him shaking his head.

"What did they say?" I ask.

"The load won't be ready until eleven a.m."

We have a couple of hours to kill, so of course our fantasies return to the elusive breakfast, coffee, and—dare we dream—a hot shower. While still in line at the security entrance, we start an internet search for a breakfast place nearby with enough parking for a truck. Our search yields a Walmart Supercenter with a Wendy's next door. Not exactly a gourmet establishment, but we'll take it.

But before we can get on our way, Mike's phone rings. The almighty aluminum gods want us to move to the back of the property, toward the loading bays, and wait there, but first we're required to drive up onto the company's weigh station. Once on the scale as instructed, we wait for lights to flash from the security building, the signal that we have registered our empty weight. We will repeat the same drill when we depart—hopefully soon—with our load. The point is to verify that we took on an extra 42,000 pounds before we leave.

Next, we climb down from the cab and enter the security house. An unusually genial security officer reminds us we'll need hard hats once we get to the loading area. Roger that. Then he dangles the carrot of a quick load. He says the plan is for us to drive to the loading dock, load up, then just wait for "lab results" on our aluminum before we take off. He suggests that this will be faster than waiting until the results are in before we start loading. While neither Mike nor I have any idea what the lab tests are about, this makes sense to us. It sounds extremely efficient. We like this security officer.

A spring in our step, we hustle to our truck and pull around back near the loading-dock area. We don our hard hats and neon safety vests, descend from the cab, and head inside to tell someone that we are here, ready, and eager. Places to go, people to see. Well, apparently, we're not going anytime soon.

We are not going to be loaded. At least not now. The older gentleman inside advises us that our load isn't ready because the lab results aren't in.

"Maybe by about eleven a.m."

It's only nine thirty. This guy we don't like so much. Chances are good that the smiling security officer simply gave us a well-worn line about being loaded fast just to convince us to move our truck out of the entrance lane. Mike has a question.

"Can we leave and come back?"

The guy says we can't and instructs us to park our rig off to the side so as not to block the bays.

To park in that position, Mike must perform what he calls offset backing, which is kind of like a parallel-parking maneuver, to angle backward in limited space near the loading bay alongside other waiting trucks. Once this is accomplished, Mike quickly falls asleep in his driver's seat.

I consider it a blessing to be able to sleep precisely when the opportunity presents itself. Mike does this at night too, hits the bunk and zonks out. I've not been graced with such a blessing. Nor does it look like I'll be blessed with a toilet in my short-term future. At least not until the magical eleven a.m. hour when we might enter the loading dock. While Mike snores thunder, I watch other trucks arrive empty and leave loaded. Four trucks, to be exact. Maybe patience isn't something I've been blessed with either.

With time on my hands, I become even more curious about why our aluminum needs lab tests. Where is this aluminum going—are we talking about soft-drink cans or beer cans? I google the name of the company we will deliver to in Wisconsin. It turns out that they aren't in the soda-can business—not even close. This aluminum, if we ever get it loaded, is headed to Uncle Sam and the U.S. military.

The company is a defense contractor; its website proudly proclaims it is "the sole producer of medium caliber cartridge cases—20mm, 30mm and 40mm—for the U.S. Department of Defense."

We're talking bullets, not beer cans. They make cartridge cases for the ammunition used in gun systems in Apache helicopters and CH-160 helicopters; the A-10 Thunderbolt II Close Combat Gunship, or Warthog; the LPD-17 naval vessel; and even for high-velocity grenade launchers. In the span of just an hour, Mike and I have gone from helping supply the home-building industry to helping bolster American soldiers for battle.

At 11:40 a.m. we get a knock on the driver-side door. I rouse

Mike. They are ready for us. The soaring door to bay number 2 opens and Mike skillfully backs the rig into the narrow loading dock. As we drop out of the truck, we're told to start setting up mandatory safety rails along the sides of our flatbed. How nice of them to show concern for our safety. But it doesn't take long for us to realize that the safety rails aren't to protect us; they're for the two workers who will stand on our trailer, eyes fixed upward, and methodically maneuver the long, heavy stacks of aluminum rods with a remote-controlled crane.

An hour later, our load tarped, tied, and tight, we pull out and start the more-than-ten-hour trip from central Ohio to Antigo, Wisconsin. Mike plans not to stop for the night until we are somewhere north of Chicago, not necessarily because he'll run out of legal drive time but because he's thinking ahead to tomorrow. Long-haulers are always thinking two or three days ahead. He wants to go as far as we can today so he can minimize drive time to our drop site tomorrow. That will increase the chances that he can drop off this load, be assigned another one, pick it up, and get on his way all in the same day. Mike aims for less than four hours of driving in the morning to Antigo so he'll still have seven hours of legal drive time left for another load. As always, he's chasing that next load and the cash that comes with it.

Mike isn't happy. He senses we are running behind. He needs five loads a week to reach his money goals. We might not get there with these delays. So Mike explains we'll "steal time" from the next load and the next until we catch up and can take additional loads. Mike reminds me that his company strives for

$2,000 a day gross per truck. Today, our aluminum represents $2,800 gross for the company. We just need to get it to its destination. Mike is confident.

"Something kicks in when I'm behind."

It's the will and the thrill to load faster, stop less, keep driving with a taped hose, push the envelope of remaining fuel in hopes of the reward that comes with the next load. There's a trucker phrase that embodies that spirit: "Risk it for the biscuit."

I hear Mike say it often.

Mike wants to get as much drive time in tonight as reasonably possible. It's seven o'clock Wednesday night—past the time to find an open spot at a major truck stop. The Trucker Path app confirms that all spots are full at the next Pilot. I really want a place with a shower. But Mike enlightens me on the correlation between showers and earnings.

"If I hit four thousand in a week, I guarantee you I haven't showered. That's a tough week, a rare week. Also, I don't like paying for showers at these mom-and-pop truck stops when I know my company gets them for free at certain big-name stops." Whenever I bring up showers, toilets, toothbrushing, Mike replies, "We live like animals out here."

Mike and I finally come to rest at a vast, shiny, revamped truck stop near Racine, Wisconsin. It is a Petro stop, owned by TravelCenters of America—self-described as "the largest publicly traded full-service truck-stop company" in the country. Corporate revenue is over ten billion dollars a year across 270 locations in the United States and Canada. They also own the TA truck stops you've seen along the interstates, and they used to control the Quaker Steak and Lube restaurants right off the highways. It's an intriguing operation, but it isn't a Flying J or a Pilot, places where employees of Mike's company enjoy member benefits and credits. Because of this, Mike isn't thrilled with where we find ourselves, but maybe he's sensed my desire to check out a big-time stop—and grab a shower.

Or maybe it's fate. I will later learn more about this truck stop from an entirely different perspective—from victims who were trafficked there. We are also just fourteen minutes from where Rebecca Landrith was last seen before she was shot twenty-six times by trucker Tracy Ray Rollins last year.

Mike hasn't been at this stop since they underwent a major remodel, but he's heard good things. The Trucker Path app tells us that plenty of the 185 parking spots are still open—which is strange, given the late hour. Once we pull in, we find out why. Their spots aren't free—none of them. It costs fifteen bucks for the night. The first two hours are free, presumably for drivers who just want to shower, have a meal, take a nap, or, maybe, have a "commercial" guest.

It looks like we are paying a premium for a fancy truck stop. This doesn't sit well with Mike. In fact, he doesn't want to pay. But I am ready for a clean toilet, a hot shower, and a sit-down meal, which are all vanishing before my eyes. Plus I want to see this operation. I tell Mike I'll spring for the fifteen-dollar fee. Big spender.

I watch Mike's expression as we walk in. He's a big kid in a big candy store. He stops in his tracks, takes it all in, then starts telling me what the place used to look like before the major renovation and expansion. I am impressed too. This place is vast. It has a grocery store with cheese and meat cases. There's a wine and spirits aisle—which strikes me as a bit odd, since U.S. DOT regulations prohibit truckers from having alcohol anywhere in their tractors. You can buy a whole bottle of Tito's or a nice cabernet here, but what will you do with it if getting caught means an automatic violation?

The showers are fourteen bucks each, and paying that will violate Mike's deeply held convictions. He tries haggling a bit with the well-seasoned lady behind the counter, looking for a discount and getting her to see if his old account with Petro is still active (it isn't). Eventually, we pay up. She hands us our tickets, which have numbers that will be called over the PA system, indicating which of the many private shower rooms are now clean and blissfully ours. It's been a long time since I appreciated a simple hot shower and clean bathroom as much as this.

After our showers and a change of clothes, Mike and I make our way upstairs to check out the Blue Badger restaurant. In addition to table seating, there's a long wraparound bar. Truckers of all shapes, ages, sizes, and colors perch at the bar, quaff beers and cocktails, and talk—not to each other but on their headsets to friends or family. It's an odd sight, a trucker version of the *Star Wars* bar scene. I also can't help noting that since it's a Wednesday night, it's unlikely that these guys are on their thirty-four-hour downtimes. Many of them will be on the roads in the morning, maybe in a few hours.

The alcohol issue prompts me to ask Mike about the minimum age to obtain a commercial driver's license. He tells me you can get a CDL at eighteen, but that's only to drive within your home state. You have to be twenty-one for an over-the-road, or OTR, license.

While it's no longer unusual to see a bar at the big truck stops, back in Dale Weaver's day, it was an exception—at least legal bars. Dale recalled a place in Wheeling, West Virginia, that had one of the first truck-stop bars he ever saw. If you walked through the bar, there was an illegal poker game in a backroom casino. At one Oklahoma City bar, Dale had a gun stuck in his face. There was this guy next to Dale, a driver from C and H with a Boston accent, who had been chatting up the lady bartender. Then her boyfriend walked in. The boyfriend assumed Dale was with the Boston guy. He aimed the gun at Dale's head and backed both the other driver and Dale right out of the bar. No wonder Dale chose to keep to himself.

Mike and I have every intention of dining at the Blue Badger, but the waitress informs us they are shutting down for the night. It's late and Mike doesn't feel like cooking in the truck. We decide—again—to Grubhub it. We check the app for what is nearby, fast, and mutually agreeable. Our food is delivered to the front door of the truck stop, and we eat our dinner alone at the empty food-court tables.

Back at the truck after dinner, Mike lets the logbook know that we are down for the night. He says truckers sometimes enter *unloading* at night even though the off-load won't happen until the next morning. This can allow them to drive longer the next day—but it can also be disproved by someone who is looking for signs of cheating.

It will be an early day tomorrow and we have a load of aluminum to deliver to Uncle Sam. It's lights-out for us.

CHAPTER 15

THE OKLAHOMA CRIME ANALYST

When I ask her about the FBI's Highway Serial Killings Initiative, Terri jokes, "I birthed it—the FBI is raising it."

She isn't wrong. She reminds me about the perpetual perception among police agencies that the FBI takes a lot, but doesn't give back. Yet Terri is quick to clarify that the perception isn't reality when it comes to the HSK. She calls the FBI program "All giving—training, information, coordination."

Still, Terri makes a candid comment about the FBI's ViCAP database: "It's always been the best idea nobody ever used."

By that she means that this incredible violent-crime resource that "allows all of law enforcement to be on the same page" is an awesome idea but not very user-friendly.

"It's too cerebral. It was designed by profilers driven by victimology analysis. The FBI says, 'Here are these volumes of questions you need to answer on this questionnaire.' No cop is going to do that."

Thankfully, today's ViCAP reporting form has been pared down and is somewhat easier to use. Yet there's still not broad law enforcement awareness.

"Even today, if you ask some departments if they're familiar with ViCAP, they'll say, 'What's ViCAP?'"

Terri dismisses the negative perceptions the murders generate about all long-haul truckers: "The vast majority of truckers are good, hardworking people. Without that industry, our nation comes to a screeching halt."

Terri's career is based on analyzing facts and data, and she knows that her claim is backed up by the statistics on trucking's role in the national supply chain. In 2021, almost eleven billion tons of freight were moved across America. But Terri has a reminder for me:

"The industry also provides a ripe environment for someone who wants to travel through multiple jurisdictions, prey on victims that no one knows are missing, and take their crime scene with them."

A crime scene on wheels.

I'd be remiss if I didn't ask a seasoned crime analyst like Terri, who has nearly forty years on the job, to share some insights and data about the victims and the suspects she's come across. She tells me, though, that conclusions don't come easily.

"Most of our victims are along a wide age range, some in their late thirties, some in their early twenties, some older. Some were pimp-controlled; most were not."

I ask Terri if perhaps it's harder for a woman to fall prey to a killer trucker if that woman is pimp-controlled.

"Yes, it's less likely because at least someone is almost always watching."

I ask if she has seen victims who were outlaws—the women who are in the business not to provide sex but to rob men. While it might sound like that scenario could trigger violence, Terri says she doesn't think she has ever seen any victims who worked as outlaws.

As for the serial-killer truckers, Terri cautions against trying to distinguish them from other serial killers. The profiles are likely the same: predominantly white males, often antisocial. "They just happen to drive a truck."

Sure, but do more killers gravitate to trucking because of the isolation and opportunities it offers? My gut tells me they do.

There was one thing Terri was certain about.

"Drugs play a huge role with both the victims and the truckers. The girls are working to pay for the dope, and the dope numbs them enough to keep working. The drivers are often using meth or coke to keep driving."

Drugs put the victim and the trucker together inside that truck; it is often the means and the method and, sometimes, even the motive. During her peak years working these cases, Terri saw drug use particularly with bull haulers—truckers who haul livestock such as cattle and have to get their precious cargo delivered on time with no harm or loss.

She fills me in about the party row that used to be in the back of big lots at the larger truck stops in the years before the internet became the venue of choice for enticing truckers and nearby massage parlors and motels became the preferred location to transact business.

"As they come into a town, truckers will set up 'dates.' They get on their CBs looking for commercial, then park in party row, positioning their rig in a certain way that illustrates they're interested in company. There'll be a knock on their window. A girl goes in—fifteen minutes later, she's out and knocking on the next truck door."

Both Terri Turner and Dale Weaver have some time and distance from the current state of affairs, but despite the physical shift away from some of the truck stops, the threat of truckers preying on vulnerable women is still a clear and present danger. Maybe even more so because it has inched closer into our communities. And at least one case involved an interesting twist—truckers who allegedly cut out the middleman by kidnapping, assaulting, and pimping out victims themselves. According to court documents filed in 2021, Brian Summerson and Pierre Washington reportedly grabbed their victims in towns along their trucking routes, beat them, and forced them into the sex trade. If a woman declined, the pair would call the victim's friends or family and demand money. The FBI issued a plea for the public's help in identifying additional victims whose images appeared on Summerson's and Washington's electronic devices.

FBI PRESS RELEASE
April 2021

MEMPHIS, TN—The FBI is asking for the public's assistance in seeking potential victims and additional information about two over the road truck drivers who kidnap females and demand ransom of the females for their release.

Brian T. Summerson, 25, of Dillon, South Carolina, was arrested in Daytona Beach, Florida, for Battery Causing Bodily Harm, False Imprisonment, and Tampering with a Witness Calling 911. Summerson is an over the road trucker with a primary route of I-95 from New Jersey to Miami, as well as

Chicago, Illinois, and Kansas City, Missouri. When meeting potential victims, he tells them his name is Von or Vaughn.

Pierre L. Washington, 35, of Chicago, Illinois, owns a trucking company, God Got Me LLC. Washington is also an over the road trucker, but at this time, his routes are unknown. Washington was arrested in Chicago, Illinois, in March 2021 by the FBI in reference to an ongoing investigation.

The investigation is ongoing and has revealed photographs, videos, and text communications of additional women on Summerson's electronic devices and electronic accounts.

The FBI places a priority on protecting victims of crime. If you have any information concerning this case, or if you believe you are a victim or may have been affected by these alleged crimes, please provide your contact information via email to truckervictims@fbi.gov so that an investigator can contact you. Your responses are voluntary but would be useful in the federal investigation and to identify you as a potential victim.

CHAPTER 16

THURSDAY WITH MIKE

I'm up at five a.m. after my first good night's sleep in three days—thank you, Petro truck stop. Mike's alarm won't go off for another thirty minutes, so I slink down from my bunk, split the magnetic mesh-curtain closure, and step into the front of the tractor to dress in the dark. Having learned my lesson from the previous early-morning searches for clothes and shoes, I've already laid out today's wardrobe on top of my duffel bag. It's all part of the choreographed routine when two people occupy a rig.

Mike and I planned last night how we'll maximize efficiency this morning. It's my job to get the coffee—there's a Dunkin' Donuts inside the food court. Mike isn't a regular coffee drinker, but he tells me he'll need the caffeine to make today's drive. He likes his jolt in the form of a large iced vanilla-flavored concoction—light and sweet. I'm a purist—medium size and black. While I get the coffee, Mike will cook a quick breakfast of scrambled eggs with turkey, peppers, and mushrooms.

It's frosty in the truck even with the heat on. There's a light mist of rain spotting the windshield. I layer my hoodie over my flannel shirt, pull on my down vest, and top it off with my black American flag trucker's cap. Cold drizzle won't deter me from the two-hundred-yard walk through the rows of slumbering, rumbling semis and into the welcoming warmth of the Petro. This is also my chance to brush my teeth over a real sink, so I shove my toothbrush and toothpaste into my vest pocket. Hot coffee awaits.

When I return, Mike is awake, dressed, and cooking up a skillet full of eggs. It looks delicious and smells magnificent. As I watch, turned sideways in the passenger seat, Mike scoops the steaming-hot scramble onto a paper plate and hands it to me. I'll wipe down the skillet once it's cooled and we're on our way. Mike pours his eggs into a big red Solo cup so he can eat while driving, his left hand on the wheel, his right hand wrapped around the cup.

We roll out of the lot and begin a three-and-a-half-hour jaunt up 41 from Racine to Antigo, Wisconsin. It's funny how quickly my concept of what a long drive is has changed. Three and a half hours? Meh.

With plenty of time to talk, Mike shares his vision for his future.

"My plan is to buy my own truck, drive it for a couple of years, buy another truck, put somebody in it, buy another one. Maybe own four or five trucks. Make some money, buy some real estate, get married, have kids."

That order is important to Mike.

"These truckers who have wives and kids—they need to find a different career."

Dale Weaver didn't have that kind of insight when he was Mike's age.

When Dale worked for Daily Express, the freight was up

east, and Dale lived in Texas. He wasn't home much. Dale had been married three times—and never longer than three years.

"Trucking and wives don't work. Wives want you home, but that truck isn't making a dime parked in the backyard. I'm a loner—have been all my life. My family was just five separate individuals under one roof—we were not close. It just doesn't work. Women think they're going to change you, or they don't realize how lonely it's really going to be."

Dale had a lady friend whom he lived with in his modular home in Glendale. But when Dale retired, she decided to move about a hundred miles away into a house she'd inherited. "We're both happier that way."

I'm concerned about Mike's lack of health insurance. Mike is an independent contractor, so he doesn't get the kind of benefits a trucker employed by a big company gets. He is required to pay $119 a month through his employer for on-the-job coverage for work-related injuries. As I get to know Mike, my gut tells me that if that OTJ injury coverage weren't mandated, he wouldn't have it. I ask Mike what happens if he gets appendicitis or a kidney stone or breaks his ankle back home.

"I'll just figure it out. I keep money in the bank for such things. And I would probably hit up family members for help, like I did recently when I needed a root canal."

There's a CB radio mounted over Mike's head, and I note that it hasn't squawked once yet. That's because it isn't turned on. Mike uses it mostly in winter for traffic and weather updates from other drivers. It cost him forty dollars—the cheapest one he could find. There's a built-in antenna in the new Volvo, so the CB is just a plug-and-play unit. Mike turns on his CB for me, but it is either not cooperating or no one out there is talking.

The radio silence is a stark contrast to the near constant chatter of truckers during the mid-1970s through much of the 1980s. By the 1970s, CBs were ubiquitous in truck cabs, but they date back decades prior. The armed forces were the first to embrace two-way citizens band radios. Then oil-field hands adopted them, followed by all manner of workers who suddenly just had to have their radios within arm's reach. Smaller, less expensive CBs became available in the 1960s, and when the price of gasoline spiked and fuel was scarce during the 1973 oil embargo, truckers started squawking over the air when they spotted the rare open gas station or, even rarer, cheap gas. It didn't hurt that truckers also took great pleasure in tipping each other off about state troopers—Smokeys—up ahead.

The resolution of the oil embargo didn't stop truckers' affection for their radios. In fact, the government added even more channels to make room for all the drivers who now knew one another by their handles—nicknames like Snake and Mongoose—and passed the time exchanging road stories, diner reviews, and family updates like members of an interstate coffee klatch.

Today, with apps and social media, digital movies, cell phones, and headsets, it's hard to discern the sense of a collaborative community of truckers just from listening to the airwaves.

Mike observes that lots of truckers pass the time on long hauls by watching movies while they drive. The next time a big rig sways into my lane, I'll wonder if the driver is caught up in a horror flick or an action film. Many truckers also listen to satellite radio, some all day.

But Mike chooses to chat on the phone. He stays in almost constant communication with buddies, family members, dispatchers, the boss man, Japanese car-parts sellers—all on his phone headset. During one conversation, I overhear Mike, the former kitchen ace, converse dreamily about the pluses and minuses of pistachios in honey-soaked baklava. On the other end of the culinary call is Mike's older brother, who lives in Thailand. Mike signs off the call with some brotherly affection: "I love you, man."

All this time on the phone makes it unlikely that Mike—or another trucker who chats this much—is a killer. His cell phone would constantly ping off the nearest towers and eventually be traced to the crime scene.

I asked old Dale Weaver how he'd passed the time through the years. Since he wasn't much of a talker, he chose to immerse himself in books on tape to pass the endless hours on the road. I heard his love for books in his voice.

"There's no way for me to even estimate how many books on tape I've listened to over the years. If you get a good book and a great reader, you don't even want to stop for a piss."

Now that's the kind of book review that I want.

I listen as Mike, on the phone, coaches newer drivers who call him with their crises of the moment. While I am with him, Mike fields a call about a near jackknife incident.

Flatbeds don't handle tight turns or U-turns as well as dry vans do. In fact, they don't really handle them at all—they jackknife. Flatbeds have split axles, which make those turns tough on the axles and the tires. That why Mike makes extra-wide turns. It strikes me how very wide a radius we need to execute what seems like a relatively easy turn. We use the whole road. That often means waiting agonizingly long times for traffic to clear in all directions, especially in the lanes alongside us, so we don't take out a car or two when we swing wide right in order to turn left.

Mike takes a call from a newer trucker who needs advice about a log violation. He tells Mike he hadn't paid attention to his log indicator that displayed the time remaining until a mandatory break. When Mike's friend exceeded the maximum eight hours of driving without a break, his logbook flashed and alerted him and recorded a violation.

"What do I do? I have a violation now?"

Mike calms his colleague and explains that the violation will remain in his log for only seven days. If there is no other violation of any kind—if he doesn't get pulled over, inspected, and dinged for anything else—the break-time violation will vaporize. Of course, this means he must ride clean and pristine for the next week—not a scenario for the fainthearted or angst-ridden.

Inspections come in three varieties. Level three is a low-level check—they check your logbook and license. For level two, they look at your tires and your load and take a walk around your rig. Level one is like a proctologist's probe. The inspectors open your hood, hook up to your computers, and check your fluid levels.

Mike sees this as a teachable moment for the less experienced trucker. He tells him that there are ways to minimize the odds of being written up for something on an inspection and thereby lower the chances of activating the break-time breach that silently lurks in the log. A trucker can pay a mechanic at a truck stop ten bucks to check the air on each tire and air up to the correct PSI. This can avert the disaster of being stopped and cited for improper tire pressure during a DOT inspection. A long-hauler might even pay a mechanic to conduct the equivalent of a level one, two, or three DOT inspection and correct whatever needs to be fixed. This brings you the peace of mind of knowing you would pass if the real thing happened, that you won't cost your company a ding and some money and get a mark on your own record.

But of course, a preemptive inspection costs not only money but valuable time on the road. There's always a cost-benefit analysis to the long haul. Your other option is to just cross your fingers and "risk it for the biscuit."

After spending so much time poring over pages of morbid details of murder and mayhem committed by serial-killer truckers, I find it almost refreshing to listen to a long-hauler anxious about getting in trouble for forgetting to take a break.

Mike gets another call from a buddy who needs a tutorial on the appropriate use of a log entry known as *adverse conditions*. I listen and learn as Mike explains that this category of log entry is often abused. It's a way drivers make up for lost time and drive longer than allowed—they claim, falsely, that really bad weather or almost totally stalled traffic caused them to drive much slower.

Hitting the *adverse conditions* entry subtracts drive time from the daily maximum hours for the duration of the conditions. But an inspector or trooper who sees that log entry can easily refute it. "Hey, there was no rainstorm yesterday." Or

"There was no blizzard this morning." Or "There was no hour-long traffic jam last night."

Misusing it is cheating, Mike tells his colleague.

In just the single week I spend with Mike on the road, we experience multiple near misses with other vehicles. From my passenger-seat perch, I watch in alarm as clueless automobile drivers think nothing of quickly cutting in front of us, where they vanish from view somewhere in the black hole below our grille. There are those who, thinking they possess superpowers, attempt to pass us on the right just as they emerge from an entrance ramp, trying desperately to match the full speed we've already committed to.

Mike makes use of his horn for various levels of warning. There is the happy horn: a light soprano pitch that says, *Go ahead, I'm letting you in the lane,* or acknowledges a waving kid in a passing car. Then there's the heavy horn, a basso profundo that rattles internal organs. That's the sound reserved for imminent threat to life and limb. It works, at least during our week together. But Mike, like other truckers, has some harrowing scenes permanently residing in his memory. I ask him to share what he can.

Mike has to prepare himself to tell me this story; there's a deep breath involved.

"I was a brand-new driver. It's a rural country roadway in Kentucky, tiny homes on either side. It's after dark and there's a deluge of rain, almost no visibility. In my rearview mirror, I see a GMC Yukon racing up from behind me. It's going way too fast. I'm like, 'Is this guy out of his mind?'"

The "big, stupid SUV"—as Mike calls it—moves to pass Mike on the left. The driver is going to cross a double solid yellow line, and he can't see what's about to happen. But Mike sees. Mike knows, and he is helpless to stop it. The Yukon slams head-on, at full speed, into a much smaller oncoming car. It happens in a split second, but to Mike, it plays out as if it's a slow-motion scene in a horror flick. Before Mike fully registers the tragedy he just witnessed, he is many yards past the accident, and he is a wreck himself. His body shakes as he tries to control his rig. Questions surge into his mind: *Should I stop? Could I even stop my truck now in this downpour? How long would it take me? Are there cars on my tail that will hit me if I start applying the brakes? Can those cars stop before they hit me? Would that cause another accident? What help can I offer corpses, which these people now surely are?*

Mike checks his rearview and confirms several cars have slowed around the scene. He keeps rolling but his body doesn't stop shaking for miles.

By week's end, Mike and I will drive that very same cruel Kentucky road.

There's another memory that Mike hasn't yet erased—and might never erase. He spots a car that rolled multiple times and landed on its side, impaled through its windows by a tree. Strangely, it looks like the car has always been wrapped around the tree, like the tree just grew right through the car. The first responders arrive on the scene but show no sense of urgency. They know what Mike already surmised—no one needs to be rescued. It's too late.

Old man Dale witnessed five decades' worth of crashes. Dale

told me about an accident where four or five people were killed. One car rear-ended another; bodies were all over the road. That happened in Nevada, where there was no speed limit at the time. It was the second deadly accident Dale witnessed in Nevada. The highway signs back then read something like USE SPEED APPROPRIATE FOR CONDITIONS.

They should have read USE SPEED APPROPRIATE FOR SURVIVAL.

As Mike and I roll closer to Antigo, Wisconsin, a vast farming and lumbering region—not to mention a big producer of ammunition casings—we navigate local roads far from any interstate. I'm treated to a close-up, drive-by look at a bygone era. Life moves slower here, and so do we.

I spot more than one unretouched original A and W drive-in restaurant. When I see the first one, I figure the faded old place must be closed, abandoned long ago. I am wrong. People are parked in their cars, placing their lunch orders. I flash back to my childhood, where a Saturday-night special treat meant the whole family piled into the station wagon, pulled up to the drive-through, and ordered hot dogs, onion rings, and the famous icy-cold root beer, all of which were delivered by a carhop waitress on roller skates. Our entire order would be perilously poised on her tray and hooked onto the rolled-down window on the driver's side of our Cadillac Sedan DeVille. I doubt they still use the roller skates here, but they do still have the original A and Ws.

We snake our way through the quiet country towns, past ancient A and Ws and Dairy Queens, and into Antigo. I always associated long-haul trucks with highways. That's true, but quite often pickups and off-loads—especially for the manufacturing industry—aren't right off the exit ramp. I also assumed that all the victims of killer truckers were in the sex trade and therefore the remainder of America could rest easy at night, safe from the threat of murderous truckers. I was wrong about that.

Adam Leroy Lane parked his truck in a working-class neighborhood outside Boston. It was summer 2007, just weeks after Detective Postiglione arrested Sarah Hulbert's killer, Bruce Mendenhall, at a Nashville truck stop. Lane set off on foot through the dark yards of homes as the nighttime temperatures plummeted about twenty degrees from the day's high. Perhaps the chill in the air was just the weather, or maybe it was the evil emanating from Lane. Lane tried the door at Kevin and Jeannie McDonough's house and found it unlocked. The McDonoughs were drifting into sleep when they heard what Jeannie described to the press as "a whimper." It sounded like it came from their fifteen-year-old daughter's room.

Mr. and Mrs. McDonough made their way down the hall and discovered a man in a mask pressing a knife to their daughter's throat. Kevin pounced on the dark figure and wrapped his arm around the man's throat. The two fell to the floor, and Jeannie yanked the knife away from Lane.

Police reports offer a clue to what Lane intended that night. When they searched him, they found Lane was carrying "three knives, a length of wire, and a martial arts throwing star." A search of Lane's truck was even more telling. In his cab, Lane kept a DVD of *Hunting Humans*—a tale about a serial killer.

"I just want to make sure this guy is on your radar." That's the message a Massachusetts state trooper sent to the FBI. Just a few months earlier, the trooper had attended an FBI presentation in Reno about the HSK Initiative. That alert trooper's concern allowed the FBI to link Lane to unsolved homicides in two more states. Lane's guilty plea in the McDonough case sent him away for five decades. The HSK Initiative worked.

As I'd expect for a Defense Department ammunition maker, the pickup site is ringed with chain-link fencing topped with barbed wire. Yet, when I take a closer look, I conclude there's no way they make finished rounds here. There can't be any gunpowder anywhere—the security isn't tight enough. If they were completing the rounds here, filling the cartridges with powder, this place would look like Fort Knox. We pull up to a side gate and call the delivery number on the big sign. I want Mike to announce that we're here with the pizza delivery, but I'm not sure these folks will appreciate the humor.

The gate electronically opens to reveal a big brown expanse of dirt—not a paved lot, just soft dirt. Soft, like maybe it rained here a couple of days ago. We wonder aloud why the sole purveyor of medium-caliber ammo for the United States Department of Defense can't afford to pave their loading lot so 80,000-pound rigs won't sink in it.

A middle-aged woman appears out of nowhere and instructs us to prepare for off-load. When Mike asks her if we should call her when we're done, she says it isn't necessary.

"I'll know when you're ready and come back out for you."

There aren't any windows looking out over the back lot, so I figure she'll know when we're ready via security cameras. It takes me a while to spot the clever concealments, but eventually I confirm we are being watched. We stage our rig on the edge of the lot, dismount, and start to untarp our load of aluminum.

Sure enough, the same woman soon appears and tells us she'll open the roll-up bay door and have us back up into the loading dock. This is the tightest spot I've seen yet. It requires Mike to pull forward onto the outer corner of the dirt lot—the softest part. Our front wheels sink slowly but surely into the moist soil. I have visions of digging our way out of Antigo, Wisconsin. But carefully, Mike shifts into reverse, angles backward onto terra firma, and doesn't stop until we are snugly ensconced inside the loading dock. The bay door rolls down in front of our grille as if to say, *You're Uncle Sam's now—at least until you're off-loaded.*

The woman who let us in, now with a male partner, starts to guide a remote-controlled crane over the top of our trailer and begin a methodical, snail-paced, rod-by-rod off-loading process. Now I have some time to kill inside an ammo-manufacturing defense contractor. I wander toward the edge of the shop floor where skilled technicians stand at workbenches inspecting individual shell casings.

Once I'm back near the truck, I step outside and onto a platform overlooking a large dumpster piled high with metal cylinders—discarded ammo casings—many of them bigger than my hand. Some have spilled onto the ground. Mike steps out too, and I explain exactly what we're looking at. His eyes widen.

"I'm taking one of those. Before we leave here, I'm taking one of those."

"You'll be on camera," I say, pointing out the concealed lens right behind us.

"Then I'm just going to ask for one."

Back inside, I watch Mike start chatting with the woman who's been running the remote crane. People skills. As the off-loading process winds down, Mike makes his move.

"What's it going to take to maybe get one of those shells from the dumpster?"

The woman tells Mike to wait a minute. Then she disappears into the back of the plant. The lady does us much better than the dirty dumpster discards—she emerges with two shiny, empty casings for each of us. She gives Mike a nod to motion him over to her. Quietly and quickly, she transfers the 30 mm shells to Mike. My guess is that this doesn't require such secrecy, but it makes Mike feel like he's won the lottery. The unexpected bounty becomes the subject of excited phone calls to Mike's friends once we're back on the road.

Dispatch calls with our next job. If all goes well—and that's not something I'm betting on—we're headed to Sagola, Michigan, to pick up a load of OSB—oriented strand board, an engineered wood used in construction. We have a two-and-a-half-hour drive north through timber territory to Michigan's majestic Upper Peninsula.

We're not far from where a victim I interviewed grew up. I did not plan this. I had no way of knowing when I asked Mike for a ride-along that I would later meet a trafficking survivor who worked the same Racine, Wisconsin, truck stop I would visit and was from the same part of the region that I'd ride into.

Sagola—population 1,200—is mostly in the Copper Country State Forest. There are trees as far as the eye can see, and farther. There are aspens, birches, and pines, maybe more trees than I have ever seen in one place. The ratio of trees to people seems like a million to one. There's also row upon row of much younger trees, likely a reforestation effort by the lumber-harvesting companies as an investment in their future.

We pull into the lumber-processing property and are surrounded by mountains of fresh timber still wearing its bark stacked twenty to fifty feet high. Towering cranes lift and swing gargantuan wood poles like they're pencils. A grown-up version of Lincoln Logs. We pull up to the truck entrance, check in with a guy in a booth, and are told to wait in line. I count eight trucks ahead of us—at least, that's how many I can see—and none of them are moving. This looks like hours, not minutes, of waiting. I'm already thinking like Mike, calculating that this wait time will have a direct impact on the rest of the day, the night, the week—the payout.

While in the queue, Mike decides we will pull an 8/2 split. According to the Federal Motor Carrier Safety Administration—part of the DOT—drivers who use a sleeper berth must take at least eight hours in the berth but can split that into two periods, as long as neither period is less than two hours. That means if we don't want to burn up our maximum allowable work hours, we can label the two hours we wait to load as *off duty,* combine that with eight hours of sleep later, and still meet our ten hours of mandated off-duty time. I'm impressed by the seemingly constant situational awareness required from a trucker who's just trying to get it right while still trying to make a buck.

After two hours of inching forward every ten minutes or so, a woman in her forties zips up to our door in a forklift. After checking our paperwork, she instructs us to pull up into the loading area. We are more than happy to oblige. Our turn has come. Another woman, much younger—blond hair poking out below her hard hat—pulls up in a forklift laden with OSB.

Mike wants to watch the loading process from outside, but the forklift operator tells him to stay in the truck. She carefully stacks tall, palletized pyramids, one after another, onto our trailer until it can't take any more. Finished, she hands us the paperwork that Mike's company has to forward to the broker to prove we picked up the right load. Her work is done, but ours is just starting as we drive around front to the tarping area to properly secure our load.

The DOT requires two points of securement within the first and last five feet of a load and every ten feet throughout a longer load. That's no easy task when it requires ascending a mountain of lumber, working atop the summit, and descending back down without falling. The height of these loads guarantees serious injury or worse for anyone unfortunate enough to take an unscheduled trip to the pavement. That's why this site requires truckers to buckle themselves to a body harness fastened to a soaring overhead beam looming high above the truck. If a trucker falls off while unfurling his tarps across the top of the load, the harness will sense the sharp drop, lock up, and suspend the trucker in midair until he can swim and claw his way back to his cargo.

Mike's not a big fan of the harness because it constricts his movements. Nonetheless, he inserts his limbs through the arm and leg holes, buckles up, and complies. With the help of a ladder that he keeps on the truck, he clambers up the side of the wood stack. I toss up the hundred-pound rolled tarps, and he drapes them over the top and down the edges. "Not bad for a fat man, right?"

As I watch him work on and around the rig, I think the short and squat Mike might have an advantage. Mike's center of gravity sits low on his frame and makes him less likely to lose his balance.

What Mike lacks in height he makes up for with smarts. Mike's mantra, which I hear repeatedly, is "Work smarter, not harder." For example, he figured out how to make the job easier by pre-positioning his tarp in just the right place on top of his loads so it drapes down just the right length on all sides. It's like unfurling your fresh bedsheet onto a mattress and getting it perfect every time.

There are trucks waiting for us to vacate the tarping station, so once we're done, we drive past the stations to tie down our loose tarps with straps and bungees. All around us, truckers are similarly securing their hauls—but one trucker stands out. She's the only female. (Less than 10 percent of all big-rig drivers are women.) This young woman is in the spot in front of us and already immersed in the laborious process of strapping, tarping, and securing her load.

She's tall with an athletic frame and her hair is pulled up into two buns. I note that she repeatedly springs high up off the ground as she tries, often in vain, to hook her bungees into the eyelets in the tarps. This makes her look more like a basketball center snagging rebounds under the boards than like a long-hauler. But despite her height, she struggles to insert the hooks into the holes.

This went on and on—jump and miss, jump and miss. But

as I watch, I realize it isn't the physicality of the task that's challenging her; it's the complete inefficiency of it. I've done this for only a few days, but even I understand what's wrong. Mike taught me that if you properly plan out the placement of your tarp, the row of holes, where the bungee hooks go, line up just above trailer level. No jumping needed. It might require a reach but certainly not a leap. She is needlessly wearing herself out. She positioned her tarps wrong.

I begin to wonder what her training was like or if she was trained at all. Did she choose flatbeds? Was she given a choice? Did someone deliberately set her up for failure? Before she's even halfway through, we are done, and Mike wants to start the journey to our drop site in Indiana.

Mike has let it be known, sometimes subtly, sometimes not, that he isn't convinced women make the best truck drivers. What he's certain of is that flatbed work is "man's work." That's what he tells me. The lifting of heavy tarps, the dragging of thick, heavy chains, the throwing of straps from ground level over the top of towering loads—he just doesn't see how they can do it. He's also quick to point out whenever a female driver, in a car or a truck, cuts us off or is on the phone or is in the wrong lane. "Women," he announces.

In my FBI career, of course I've seen women serve on SWAT teams and crush their male counterparts in speed, shooting, and agility training at the FBI Academy. But Mike seems wedded to his perceptions.

Mike doesn't express the same sentiments when a male driver puts people at risk, which, by my rough count, they do at least as much, if not more, than the females we encounter. He might curse the guy out, but he won't invoke gender.

Mike saw only one lot lizard in his year and a half of driving. She approached him and asked if he was accepting passengers. Mike told her, "Absolutely not," then watched from his truck as she knocked on everyone's door. Finally, he saw what looked like a seventy-year-old trucker walking to his truck with her.

Even during Dale's time, the action wasn't exclusive to the truck stops. He told me that in Bristol, Tennessee, which he frequently passed through, there were a lot of "red-light houses"—brothels. He said the places really had a red light outside. Truckers would drop their trailer at the truck stop and bobtail into town. Dale's quiet voice got even quieter as he looked down at the table. "I did partake in some of that—not a lot."

Mike's more recent experience seems to confirm the trend of fewer sex workers advertising in person at truck stops and more advertising online. With one exception—Las Vegas. When Mike was training, he and his trainer parked at a truck stop just outside Vegas, a county where prostitution is illegal. Four prostitutes openly approached his truck. Mike described them: "A variety of races and ethnicities—flesh on full display. No one seemed to care."

No one except maybe a murderer looking for women whom no one seems to care about. Women like Hannah, who, soon enough, will have her own encounters with truckers.

CHAPTER 17

THE FBI CRIME ANALYST

Linking cases to a common killer often can be less about tracing who's doing the killing and more about who's being killed and how. That's victimology, the study of the victims. If you're trying to figure whether certain clusters of killings are committed by the same person, there's more to it than matching lab tests, physical evidence, and hoping someone confesses to multiple murders.

"It's their lifestyle, their personal characteristics."

When I interview Catherine DeVane, she tells me victimology encompasses a myriad of components of a crime victim's life—and death.

"Do they spend time on the internet, social media? Do they read a lot? What do they read? Are they drug users? Do they trade prostitution for transportation or for drugs? What day of the week were they killed? What time of day? Did they have the same hair color? What was the age range in that cluster? Were their bodies disposed of in water, in a ditch, in the forest? Clothes on or clothes off—which clothes? Evidence of recent sex or not? Mutilation or strangulation?"

She says, "We want to look at the day of the week, the time of the day when they were disposed of, were they disposed of in water, were they all redheads, were they all a particular age range, so when you're talking about that victimology—it's about the victim. Let's talk about where they go, what they do, what they look like, the people they surround themselves with."

Catherine wants to know.

She explains that her work isn't any different than the work of any of the other analysts in ViCAP, but she is the team lead for the initiative focused on specific kinds of cases within that system, the HSK cases. While all the analysts have their assigned regions and work with local, state, federal, and tribal agencies, Catherine's specialty is the Highway Serial Killings Initiative. The HSK looks at specific murders in that ViCAP database that point to the highways.

Catherine grabs my attention with something I know little about, so I fire questions at her until she can't or won't answer any more. I start by asking her when the FBI realized it needed to do something about highway murders.

"We were aware of the initiative all the way back to 1993 when individuals started coming up along the highway." After 9/11 happened, that project got set aside, and the FBI started focusing on terrorism. "That's not to say that we forgot about those types of violations; it's just that the focus was redirected. It regained interest with the analysts within ViCAP in 2003." It really took off in 2004, she says, when they identified, with their state partners, a series of cases that came up along the I-40 corridor. "So we're looking at these cases and asking, 'What are we looking at?' We have victims being recovered along our major interstate systems and the state highways."

When the FBI analysts started taking a closer look at the

cases, they recognized there were some common aspects that might mean certain murders were linked.

"We were able to identify the commonalities based on dump site of the body, the victimology, the characteristics surrounding what was going on with that victim—the types of weapons, the types of bindings, so that's what we started looking at with this initiative. Are we looking at one offender? Are we looking at multiple offenders? What type of offenders are we looking at? Are these individuals who specifically travel the highways? Are they individuals who are from that particular area and it just seems that they went to the highway and decided to leave a body, or just decided as they were passing through that this was a great place to leave a body because it was in the dark of night?"

Catherine tells me there are now over 850 cases in the database that have been submitted by state and local agencies. That doesn't mean all those cases are linked to the same individual. Some of them are solved; a lot of them are still unsolved. The key is getting police agencies to enter their homicides into the ViCAP system. That's easier said than done. Catherine works hard to make agencies more aware of the magic the database can do if they give it a chance. That's why she's agreed to speak with me.

"We look for platforms," she says, "where we can speak to a large audience. We hold conferences, which are the Highway Initiative conferences. We've partnered with the behavioral analysis conference. We offer four days of free training to our law enforcement agencies to get them familiar with the types of violations we're looking at."

Catherine and her team do whatever they can to not only find the cases that could be missing pieces of the larger puzzle, but also make it easier for agencies to share the pieces they have. The team might read about cases in a newspaper article or in NLETS messages. When that happens, they reach out to that police department and offer their assistance at no cost.

So what qualifies a case for entry into the HSK Initiative—is it mere proximity to a highway or a roadway?

"The kinds of cases we take into the initiative, we're focusing on victims recovered along the major highways, whether it's a truck stop, a rest stop, a culvert. It could be a stranded motorist, a hitchhiker, a prostitute who is working those areas, and if law enforcement has identified a long-haul truck driver for one of these cases—those are included into this. Because those are the types of individuals that cross our U.S. states at a given moment. They could be in Virginia this morning and then be down in Texas by the afternoon. So we are not looking for just the unsolved; we are also looking for your solved cases. Because if an agency has identified an individual who's responsible for something that has some really unusual behavior, and law enforcement believes that this is not his only crime, that he may have other victims out there, we want those cases as well, because we're able to look at the various components of that case and take a look, and compare those against other cases we have in the system. Now we develop timelines on those individuals that can help us put an individual in a certain location at a given time. That's what we're looking at."

Catherine reminds me that infamous serial killer Ted Bundy traveled the highways—but he wasn't involved in the long-haul trucking industry. A highway connection isn't enough to get the HSK team engaged. The big rig is what makes the difference.

"And we didn't set up this initiative to focus on truck drivers; it just so happens that the suspects and the offenders—and I say suspects and offenders, they're a suspect until law enforcement has proven that they were responsible for that crime. So those individuals we see are tied to traveling the highway with a long-haul truck."

I ask Catherine if she, like the OSBI's Terri Turner, ever reaches out to the trucking community to help solve some of these crimes. Her answer is a resounding yes.

"One of our resources is the trucking industry. We have a point of contact that we can help send out some of our publicly released ViCAP alerts. It's a bulletin that we put together seeking information on a missing individual or the circumstances under which that individual went missing, or it could be unidentified remains. So if it's something we can publicly release, we've got a point of contact with someone who can send that out to all the truck stops nationwide that are out there.

"We also partner with some of the other organizations that are dealing with highways. I just had the opportunity to speak with the National Domestic Highway Enforcement Initiative. That was a wonderful platform to get that information out there to law enforcement that's not aware that this is there. There's a lot of challenges that go with this. The long-haul truck drivers are miles away before a body can be recovered. And at times, what's left behind? A body. There's no evidence, there's no witness, because if they do it in the dark of night where there's no traffic, it's a challenge for law enforcement. So we have to tap into all of the individuals who are dealing with this type of crime and the resources that can provide us with what we need to put the pieces of the puzzle together."

The differences and similarities among both the victims and the offenders are critical to connecting the dots across cases. I ask Catherine about those characteristics.

"The victims—some of the similarities we're seeing is their high-risk lifestyle. We're looking at a lot of prostitutes, but we're also looking at those victims who were just random. We've got individuals who were identified based on their MO because they wanted to kill someone; they didn't want to have sex with them—they just wanted to kill someone. So they went through the neighborhoods looking for unlocked doors or windows. The other type of offender we're looking for wanted to control life and death. They wanted to sexually assault them, they wanted to mutilate the bodies, they wanted to do whatever they could because with that individual, they are controlling the outcome of whatever is going on, they feel power.

"Now, we, as the analysts, aren't looking at why the individual did it; we partner with our profilers—they're the ones that look at why this individual did it, we're looking at where else did he do it? So we have a collaboration when we're working on these types of cases, with the behavioral analysis profilers."

I'm intrigued by what might prompt the inclusion of an FBI profiler in a particular case. Catherine explains it to me.

"When we decide to bring in a behavioral analysis profiler, it's because we, as the analysts, feel like there's something else going on here—we've got a series, we need to identify an individual, and we believe that's a resource our law enforcement partner needs to have fresh eyes. So if we've got an investigation that's gone cold on them, and we need a new set of eyes, a new perspective, what type of individual are we looking for that would have committed this series of crimes, then we involve them. If the investigating agency has made that plea right at the front, and said, you know we'd like a profiler on this—we've looked at it, we've had multiple eyes on this case, we don't know what kind of individual we're looking at, so we want some type of feedback from the behavioral analysis folks.

"To say, okay, here's what we're looking at as far as victimology, as far as where the body was dumped, there's a lot of things that go into play when the profilers are looking at a case. The entire case file has to come to their office and then we all sit down and take a look at everything that was done, interviews that were done, and then we start talking about where we go from here. So bringing in our behavioral analysis profilers is something that can be done from the law enforcement side or from the analyst side."

When I ask Catherine how she measures success and if the HSK solves cases, she doesn't hesitate to answer.

"Yes, our ViCAP analysts have assisted with hundreds of cases in this HSK Initiative. As recent as a couple of years ago. So, in 2013, one of the successes that we had, the Wyoming Division of Criminal Investigations [WDCI] entered a sexual-assault series that was going on in 2013. Two years later, in 2015, they submitted three more cases—these cases were linked by DNA. Now, at that time, in 2015, our analyst was requested to give analytical support to the WDCI, to see if we could help them identify an individual who was responsible for this sexual-assault series. Or if we could find additional cases that may link back to this.

"Our analyst did a search of the ViCAP national crime database and ended up finding another sexual assault that we believed was linked to those, and provided that as a lead to Wyoming. That case happened to be out of Riverdale, Utah. So that's where this initiative and the ViCAP national database are an important tool to use when we are working on these violations. Submit them into a system and let that system work for you—we've got lots of eyes on there. So we submitted that lead to law enforcement. And we said, this is why we believe that this case is related. We looked at the characteristics surrounding the crime out of Riverdale and offered it as a lead. Three months after we did, Riverdale was able to link that case to the Wyoming series by DNA. In 2019, Mark Burns was identified through genetic genealogy as the offender in that series.

"Our work did not stop at that point. What we then did was continue our analytical support by doing a full workup on Mark Burns. Looking at a timeline to develop on him from the day he's born to the day that he's incarcerated to the day he dies. We want to be able to put that individual in a certain spot, any day of the week, at a certain time, and say, 'Here's his MO, his modus operandi.' This is what this individual liked to do, here's the victimology we're looking at on this series, and then provide additional leads. Those timelines have come into play when law enforcement goes and interviews these individuals and they're trying to identify additional leads on their investigation." In 2020, Mark Douglas Burns was convicted and sentenced to 243 years in prison.

Catherine implores law enforcement to enter their cases into ViCAP. "It's a very important program that we have. We specialize here at Quantico in these heinous crimes—I mean, these are some of the worst of the worst. And we've got small agencies out there that have never seen what we see on a daily basis. We read these cases every single day throughout the day. So we're very familiar—all of our analysts in ViCAP are very familiar with our truck drivers. And something in a case will clue them in to say, 'Let me take a look at this individual over here and see, was he driving through that state during that time, could he have been responsible for this?' So let's take a look at his biographical summary that we put together, all of the agencies that have had contact with him, everything that we know that he likes to do to those victims, let's take a look at all of this, and say, 'Okay, this is a good potential lead, now let's offer this out to law enforcement and have them take a look at it.'"

I can hear it in her voice. Catherine genuinely wants to help. She wants police agencies across the country to show her what they have so the HSK might help connect the dots that point to the killers. It might take years to understand who did what to whom, but it will take even longer if no one analyzes the big picture.

CHAPTER 18

FRIDAY WITH MIKE

Either I'm hallucinating candy bars or we have once again passed the giant rotating BUTTERFINGER / BABY RUTH sign at the candy factory off I-294 near Chicago.

Sitting for hours on end can fog your brain. That's partly why Mike prefers the physicality of flatbeds. He likes the burst of activity that breaks up the monotony of the road. Mike can't imagine being a dry-van or refrigerated-reefer trucker who drives all day and has no part in the loading or unloading: "I'd lose my mind."

Loading is a sustained thirty-minute-or-longer physical workout that day-vanners never get. As unhealthy and sedentary as long-haul driving is, flatbedders might get these workouts a couple of times a day as they load and unload, pick up and drop off. They hoist the hundred-pound tarps in a squat thrust, climb up and down the trailer, ascend stacked loads to drape the tarps, crank up and cinch down straps and chains with a heavy crowbar, and do it all in reverse when they unload. Mike likes that aspect of his job.

Since he likes getting out of the truck, Saturdays are the worst for Mike. On Saturdays he's assigned the longest hauls before he goes down that night for his mandatory thirty-four hours.

Most flatbedders keep that same schedule. Refrigerated-reefer drivers might pick up loads of perishable food on weekends, but flatbed loads—steel, gypsum, aluminum—aren't weekend material.

Dale—the trucker who drove everything—drove reefers for fifteen years. They're refrigerated coolers on wheels. After driving for Daily Express, Dale needed a break from corporate trucking and decided to give it a go on his own again. He bought his own reefer and became his own boss. Going solo didn't mean that Dale was stress-free. Reefers came with their own built-in burdens.

With the benefit of hindsight, Dale told me he never did like reefers because all the loads were strictly by appointment. You delivered fresh food to your appointed destination on time or the load spoiled, along with your payday. If your reefer unit stopped working, you had only four to five hours to replace it. Dale knew this firsthand. When his cooling unit quit, he high-tailed it to a shop that switched in a used unit, and then, when Dale came through town on his return trip, they reinstalled his newly repaired fridge. Running reefer was a lot of strain on Dale, but the money and regular work were good, so good that Dale hauled produce cross-country for a decade and a half.

Dale's regular reefer route was from Nogales, Arizona, on Wednesdays, to Hunts Point in the Bronx, New York, by Saturday night. He always arrived on Saturday night so he could unload first thing Sunday morning. Hunts Point is home to one of the largest food-distribution facilities in the world, with hundreds of acres making up the Hunts Point Cooperative Market.

Dale even ran a California—to—Hunts Point route in that same Wednesday-to-Saturday window. He still seemed amazed by that mileage.

"That's a thousand miles a day. I just set my governor at sixty-three miles per hour and ran fifteen hours a day."

I didn't ask if that was legal back then; I just listened. After all, no one would know for sure what Dale was doing without electronic trackers.

Dale's destination in Hunts Point was always Fierman Produce Exchange at Terminal Market. He liked the consistency. "I'd worked with the same booker fifteen years and never laid eyes on him—that's fine with me."

No one ever mistook Dale for a social butterfly.

Like fruit flies swarming the market's produce, Hunts Point hookers flocked to the overnight ocean of truckers parked at the market. There was crime too. The theft and prostitution were rampant when Dale pulled into Hunts Point. He described the place as "out of control." And he added his belief that Mayor Rudy Giuliani had cleaned that up.

The high-crime environment was mostly an annoyance to Dale. He was more concerned about complying with the market's regulations on exhaust emissions. "Hunts Point had rules about running your AC or heat overnight there. You couldn't run your AC unless the temps hit eighty-five degrees or your heat unless it dropped below forty degrees."

Apparently, hookers and thieves were fine, but heat and air-conditioning were another story.

Dale's starting point in Nogales was its own impressively

vast hub for receiving produce coming out of Mexico. It was a seasonal operation that ran January through June, after which the produce business shifted to California and the San Joaquin Valley—America's produce department. In Nogales, Dale stacked his reefer high with tomatoes, watermelons, cucumbers, corn, and cantaloupe.

"You go down, meet your bird dog"—that's the guy who escorts you to your various load pickups—"and sign for the loads that dispatch assigned you. There are about fifty produce houses in Nogales. A driver might have five or six pickups from various houses in an afternoon."

That split load meant the trucks would have a partitioned mix of fruits and vegetables. All of that bounty had to be kept at precisely the right temperature and controlled climate. There was more to reefer trucking than simply steering a rolling refrigerator. That's because the driver became a part of the ripening process. Dale received daily instructions to carefully adjust the temperature so his tomatoes—or whatever fruits or veggies he hauled—would appropriately ripen as they rambled across the country.

"You might even have to ice it down—get a block of ice and have it blowing across the produce to maintain the proper moisture level. Or maybe grapes might have to be covered to prevent them from freezing."

Of course, Dale had to sample some of his cargo, and he was quick to point out what most of us already knew about artificially induced ripening: "The taste of those tomatoes wasn't worth a damn."

A temperature tracker on Dale's reefer spit out data on the

refrigeration levels at various points along his produce's path. Dale printed out that temperature data and stapled it to his paperwork to prove he made the required adjustments.

Dale's reefer loads included what truckers called swinging meat—entire sides of beef or pork carcasses. Fierman's market also had meat brokers and sheds for eggs and everything else you could imagine.

For Dale, swinging meat was a terrifying load because it hung from the ceiling of the truck and constantly shifted its weight as the rig rounded curves or climbed hills. That was 45,000 pounds of unpredictable cargo that could flip your truck in an instant.

"The biggest risk of this was on little town roads with rough shoulders or slopes—you can lose it in a heartbeat. It's also dirty work. You need to wash down your truck after the load—there's blood and gristle everywhere."

Young Mike has no experience with reefers or bananas yet, but he knows how to execute what he calls a NASCAR pit stop. That means speed is of the essence. We make such a stop on the way from Sheboygan, Wisconsin, to Brazil, Indiana. We'll pump only as much fuel as the time it takes for us to pee. Normally, it costs about $1,200 to fill up with diesel, and Mike fills up every two or three days.

There are two tanks, plus a third fifteen-gallon tank for "diesel exhaust fluid." DEF was mandated by the EPA a decade ago to reduce the dangerous emissions otherwise churned out by diesel engines. Researchers say it does a decent job. That's good, because big-rig engines run all night to power the AC or heat, refrigerator, and electricity. Some companies don't allow idling because of the environmental and fuel costs, but the alternative is to buy a generator unit at a price of $8,000. Too steep for most firms.

Mike warns me in advance that our gas-tank top-off should take about four minutes. I jog into the truck stop to use the restroom, and when I return, Mike is still at the pump—there's time to spare. I grab what must be a seven-foot-long squeegee pole out of a king-size water bucket, loft it above my head, and start speed-washing our windshield clear of bug guts and road debris. There's even time to hit the tall side-view mirrors and the driver- and passenger-side windows. On cue, we both jump back into the tractor. Four minutes on the dot—$500 on the fuel pump.

Keeping your truck clean is part of good trucker practice and culture according to Mike. He washes his rig once a month, more when the winter roads are coated with sand and salt.

Old Dale Weaver echoed this advice.

"I kept a clean truck, a clean-shaven face. Inspectors can tell when there's a problem—grease on the truck, worn-down brakes. But a good record pays off. After about a year of good inspections, you're more likely to get that green light when you pass an inspection stop or weigh station."

Young Mike shares his own simple truths and rules of the road that he says make the company name on his door look good:

1. Don't empty your pee jug at a truck stop.
2. Flash your lights to thank another trucker who lets you into his lane. (Flashing your lights can also mean

"Thanks for nothing," like a luminescent flip of the middle finger.)

3. Don't be seen at a bar the night before you're driving.
4. Don't put obscene slogans or stickers on your truck, like the FUCK JOE BIDEN flag we saw flying from a rig.
5. If you have time at a loading station, help a fellow trucker fold up his tarps.

Our path to Brazil, Indiana, where we'll drop our engineered wood, is flanked by corn. Cornfields, to be exact, as far as the eye can see. There are green farms dotted with grazing cows and horses whose coats gleam a brilliant brown in crystal spring sunlight. Truly beautiful American countryside abounds in all directions.

As we near Brazil, dispatch calls about a possible pickup nearby for delivery to San Antonio, Texas. I am instantly happy at the prospect of getting somewhere closer to home as my week with Mike nears an end. When I embarked on this adventure, I didn't know where we'd be when the time came to depart. I just remained flexible on timing and location and hoped for the best.

Unfortunately, Mike doesn't like what he hears about the weight of our proposed load. It's a steel coil that the broker first posted at 46,000 pounds, but then the broker informed dispatch it was 48,000 pounds, "plus or minus." That risk pushes us over our total legal weight. It could also mean not being able to fill our fuel tanks. The load sounds to Mike like the kind that usually requires a truck with an additional axle to bear the extra weight. He calls the boss man for an opinion.

The boss man is not inclined to take the load, but in a display of his trust in Mike, he leaves it to Mike to decide. It's a big decision with a potentially big payday, but it doesn't take Mike long to do the right thing and decline the coil. How many truckers will risk the weight for the money? How many owners will let them? In a flash, my trip toward home vaporizes. Texas is a no-go—at least for now—and dispatch cancels the already booked load.

The dispatcher negotiates some money out of the broker for the bad initial posting. Later, the dispatcher tells Mike that the company got $150 for the canceled job. That meant Mike's cut was $45. That's called TONU money. Short for "truck ordered, not used." That coil will have to be hauled by someone else, but there is another one in our future.

Dispatch advises that after we drop off the wood in Brazil, Indiana, we will deadhead two and a half hours to Ghent, Kentucky, pick up a giant steel coil, and haul it to Bryan, Texas. That will put me close enough to where I need to end my week. Maybe my road time with Mike will end without the need for a flight from some distant locale after all. I pull out my phone and help calculate our drive time to the Kentucky site and then on to Texas. Mike cautions me about getting too excited; we don't know how long loading will take, and since we started very early this morning, Mike's concerned we will come perilously close to hitting his maximum drive time and get trapped somewhere, unable to drive legal.

Heading west on Route 36 along the Ohio River in Jefferson County, we pass through the quaint downtown of Madison, Indiana. The place is the perfect pairing of original architecture inhabited by new businesses. It's Friday night, and hardworking citizens mark the occasion at outdoor cafés, craft breweries, coffee roasters, and their favorite watering holes in refurbished spaces from decades past. I want to join them, but a coil awaits us across the border in Kentucky.

Most flatbedders consider heavy metal coils their most dangerous load. Mike keeps some six-by-six lumber strapped to the front of the trailer in case he gets a load that isn't palletized. He positions that lumber where a load will be set down on top of it so a forklift has room to slide under the load when off-loading. And when placed between a load and the cab, the six-by-sixes serve as potentially lifesaving speed bumps in case whatever we're carrying goes rogue and attacks us from behind.

This route puts us in the same spot, on the same Kentucky road, where Mike witnessed the almost certain fatality in his rearview mirror. I understand how it played out. The rural road lined with simple homes is even narrower than I imagined. I see the double yellow line; I envision the deluge of nighttime rain, the dark slick pavement, the crashing clash of steel on steel. I'm relieved when we roll beyond it.

"If you have to break out the chains, you're getting dirty—you'll need a shower that night." That's what Mike says about the big, heavy, high-paying loads that require extra securement. It turns out the chains will roll out tonight. As for the shower—that never happens.

In the late afternoon, we arrive at a vast, sprawling steel plant in Ghent, Kentucky. After pulling up to one entrance gate and being directed to yet another down the road, we are advised that our paperwork isn't quite right. We're missing a five-digit

number that has to start with 91. Mike's papers display a verita-
ble math class's whiteboard full of numbers—but 91 isn't one of
them. Without that number, we're told, we'll be stuck in Ghent
until morning.

They direct us farther down the road to a small trailer with
a bank of phones in it. I figure maybe that's the time-out trailer,
where troublesome truckers get sent to serve detention. From
there, Mike calls a number posted on the wall and pleads his
case with a lady on the other end. Mike reads off all the various
numbers that appear on his paperwork, but I see from the look
on his face that he might as well be reciting the nuclear-launch
codes. He hangs up, and we step out of the trailer as dusk de-
scends.

This doesn't look good. Mike calls dispatch, who calls the
broker who gave us this load. Dispatch connects Mike directly
to the broker. The call is on speaker so I can hear. The dispatcher has not a clue of what a 91 number is. This makes no
sense to me. We are standing at one of the largest steel plants in
the nation. Trucks come and go at all hours ferrying steel out of
the plant. Mike has been here before. The same brokerage must
have matched a thousand loads to drivers at this plant, maybe
every day. How can the broker match a job but not include the
magical 91 number in Mike's paperwork? The broker has never
heard of a 91 number—really? The call gets us nowhere.

As we stand outside the trailer on a patch of Kentucky
bluegrass, I point out a door in the ground labeled TORNADO
SHELTER—TRUCK STAGING LOT. It's a portal to an underground bunker. Mike reaches down and opens it. Steps lead
down to a large concrete room. We joke that we might have to

spend the night down there if we don't clear up the 91 number snafu. It is getting darker, and so are our prospects.

We walk back to the truck and Mike searches his app for nearby truck stops to spend the night. There aren't any within a reasonable distance.

Mike's phone rings. I hear a female voice on the other end telling us to come back to the gate. As best we can tell, the clueless guy at the brokerage has worked this up the chain and found someone who came up with a 91 number and passed that number on to the plant.

Once inside the gates of the plant we find ourselves surrounded by thousands of steel coils. They sprout like metal mushrooms on a field of asphalt waiting for harvest. I can't help but notice that almost none of this precious product is covered. They can be rained on, snowed on, hailed on. Since we are about to spend an hour carefully covering and securing our coil cargo, I ask Mike why we're bothering. His answer is interesting.

First and foremost, Mike's paperwork says the load must be tarped, so tarped it will be. If a coil is damaged in transit, it won't be our fault. But Mike also tells me he asked the same question his first time here.

"I was told that this company's competitors are interested in knowing which types of coils are headed in which direction, and they would love to scrape a shaving off a coil that can give away its composition."

This is intellectual-property protection—a large part of my professional career. Mike is speaking my language.

Dale Weaver also divulged his brushes with secrecy—both corporate and government.

"When I was driving double-drop lowboys for C and H, the U.S. government contacted us. They found me at a truck stop in New Jersey. These government types came to my location and dropped off what looked like a communications trailer and escorted me with two black SUVs all the way to White Sands, New Mexico. There were three guys in each of the SUVs. They never said a word about what I was hauling. I figure those guys were DOD or FBI or something like that.

"I've had loads that had secret stuff on it. One time, at a manufacturing facility where they made double-knit fabric pants in Orangeburg, South Carolina, I had to put my hands over my eyes on the way to the men's room so I wouldn't see the secret manufacturing process."

Dale made me wonder whether China ever succeeded in purloining America's proprietary fabric formula, relegating millions of its citizens to a future filled with plaid polyester.

Mike's trailer audibly groans under the weight of the coil painstakingly lowered into place by a gargantuan overhead crane. The lumber he pre-positioned to serve as bumpers on each side of the coil cracks as the load settles in. My eyes widen as I check to see if our tires show any signs of strain. Nope.

As with each of Mike's loads, we send photos to the boss man to confirm how we wrapped and secured it. I became the official photographer. Mike is particularly proud of this load job, so I take progressive photos, first to show our use of six chains, then another with the tarps wrapped tightly over the tubular coil in a custom fit worthy of a Savile Row tailor, and then a final photo with the straps crisscrossed over the whole enchilada. Our coil looks like a Christmas colossus or a birthday present for Iron Man. Mike transmits my photos to the boss man via Viber, an encrypted app like WhatsApp.

Despite all the glitches and delays of the week, Mike will still pocket his target payout figure.

We finish loading and securing at 9:30 p.m. Next we have to weigh out as we exit the grounds. Here, this is an efficient, contactless process. We drive onto the scale and the truck is electronically scanned to confirm our identity and our destination. Mike grabs a receipt from a machine outside his window that looks like an ATM on steroids. In front of us, a digital display proclaims our gross weight: 78,280 pounds.

CHAPTER 19

SATURDAY WITH MIKE

The Gorilla Tape performs above and beyond the call of duty. I wonder if they keep a roll of this miracle maker on board SpaceX rocket ships, just in case. Mike still plans to get the new hose installed during his thirty-four hours of downtime this weekend. He also needs a 20,000-mile oil change. That doesn't sound much like time off to me. We and our precious coil are pointed toward a new Texas destination near Houston after spending last night in a parking lot at the Kentucky steel plant.

Near Greenwood, Kentucky, a pickup truck tries to pass us even though Mike was signaling a lane change for the last quarter mile. Mike lays on his horn as we veer to avoid disaster. I glance into the pickup and observe the inevitable—the driver's eyes are fixed on a cell phone in his right hand. He's totally clueless as to how close he just came to a life-changing—or life-ending—experience. Yet another near miss has me asking why we call our devices smartphones when drivers who use them are anything but.

Speaking of smart, Mike recruited his college-educated friend Ricardo to Ox and Eagle and trained him to drive. Ricardo holds a degree in physical therapy. Like many Americans, Ricardo is burdened with serious student-loan debt. He knows he needs a master's degree to get anywhere in PT, but that means even more debt. He's tired of being broke. That's why Mike told Ricardo how he could make six figures after just six weeks of CDL classes.

The phone chirps. It's Ricardo, who is driving in Memphis, Tennessee. Someone in a car just pointed a gun at him while trying to speed ahead on a highway entrance ramp. I listen to Mike's end of the conversation and don't understand why Ricardo's first call is to Mike and not 911. My twenty-five years in law enforcement kick in.

I implore Mike to convince Ricardo to call 911 with a description of the driver and vehicle. It takes a lot of cajoling, but Ricardo agrees to do it. I'm relieved; this driver is clearly a menace, and he is going to hurt someone. Surely the police will find the driver and arrest him for the threatening display of a weapon.

I am wrong. The police tell Ricardo they won't do anything unless he stops his truck, waits for an officer, and provides an in-person statement. I'm beside myself. Time is money. Truckers won't stop, wait forever for an officer, and provide a statement when they know the other driver is probably already in another state. There's no sense ruminating on this when I can focus on something new—like our gas gauge.

We have a quarter tank of gas left. Company rules say we must refuel. If you run out of gas, air gets in the lines; someone has to come out and pump diesel back into the system and that person charges six dollars a gallon to do it. Time and money. I remark to Mike that he seems to know quite a bit about that process. He confirms he is speaking from experience. We fill up at a Pilot station. It's an eight-minute pit stop that also allows us to check on the coil load—all is good.

Back inside the cab, we have more time to talk about challenging loads—loads that when mishandled present a danger to the driving public. Mike tells me how he almost hauled loose pipes that were inserted within larger pipes. The client loaded the heavy cargo on Mike's trailer, which gave him a closer look at what they had done. The pipes were nestled inside other pipes, tied together only with metallic twine. This meant the inner pipes could slide in and out and do their own thing. Mike balked. The client pushed back. The ensuing debate took a long time to resolve.

"We always do it this way," the client said.

Mike didn't really care much about tradition. "How much weight do you think that metal twine you're using is rated for? I'll tell you: none. Twine isn't for securing loads."

The client finally agreed to reconfigure the load for Mike.

But that means other truckers are on the road with pipes that can slide loose while they're climbing a hill and fire out of the larger pipes like mortar rounds out of a cannon. That's something to think about the next time I find myself behind a truck that's hauling pipes. On second thought, I will never find myself behind a truck hauling pipes for more than the time it takes me to change lanes.

Mike's account of the perilous pipes makes me wonder why there aren't more level-two and level-three inspections. Like everything in trucking, I'm sure it's all about time and money. Not enough government funding for inspectors, big corporate trucking interests lobbying against the loss of road time, and big players balking about fines and citations.

Since we're on the general topic of safety, I ask Mike about drug testing.

"There is random urine testing for drugs. I was tested twice this year. Some drivers in my company have yet to be tested. But a trucker gets two weeks' notice of a drug test to allow for travel plans back to the lab in Chicago."

That lead time might give drivers enough room to try and flush something out of their systems. Mike's also been subjected to a random Breathalyzer test, which he thought was kind of silly because of the early heads-up he was given. When he was first told of an "alcohol test" he thought maybe it would be a precise blood test, but it was just "a blow-in-a-tube thing."

We pass through the town of Horse Cave, Kentucky, population 2,200—more if you include all the truckers parked around the massive mega-mall adult establishment alongside the highway. Signs over the big gravel lot advertise plenty of truck parking and "videos, private booths, and more." The *more* part troubles me. We look it up on Trucker Path. Mike scrolls through some of the comments and mutters, "Filthy, disgusting."

There are posts from truckers looking for gay hookups: *"Looking for fun." "I'm here now." "Can a straight guy find fun?" "I'll be stopping at 9 p.m."*

I wonder who might be trafficked here. Is a killer trucker parked here right now searching for a victim? What would it take for Horse Cave to shut places like this down?

(Six months later, I learn the answer to my question. In September 2022, a business called the Horse Cave Adult Bookstore agreed to close after a three-year police investigation and undercover operation. Over the years, the Hart County Sheriff's Department had cited the place more than thirty times and charged several people for indecent exposure. The investigations included examining how two people died in the video-arcade area known as the back room. The sheriff claimed sex acts were performed inside the establishment and illegal substances were sold. Three years and two deaths—that's what it took for a community to rid itself of a drug-infested death trap.)

In a blink, Horse Cave is behind us. Soon my week with Mike might be too. This seems like a good time to solicit Mike's thoughts on which truckers are more likely to kill—who are these men who bring such dishonor to an honorable profession? I ask this question of everyone I interview, and now it's Mike's turn.

Mike traces a direct line from personality to truck type. He outright rejects any notion that the kind of truckers who choose flatbeds are serial killers. Flatbeds mean greater engagement—with the load, with dispatchers, and with the clients on either end of the load. The personality type of a flatbedder, Mike theorizes, is more social, less likely to kill. The whole process of loading and securing, the physicality of it, and the mental acuity it requires, argues against the ruminating, obsessed, disengaged loner that Mike pictures as a killer. The built-in physical engagement with flatbedding and, to some extent, with tanker trucks breaks up the mounting monotony of the relentless road. Mike is squarely pointing at the dry-van guys. Maybe Mike should moonlight as a crime analyst.

While Mike's theory at first sounds self-serving—*Hey, it's not me*—it does make sense.

And although he didn't choose to run flatbed, it's clear to me after a week with Mike that pulling a dry van would drive him crazy and cause him to ask for more action. We pause our theorizing for a moment to ponder my imminent reality: I need to get home.

Saturday is decision time. Something has to give, as I need to be back home in the next twenty-four hours. We just entered Tennessee and are looking at another thirteen hours of driving to drop off the coil on Monday morning in Houston. Mike faces his mandatory downtime soon—no more driving no matter where he finds himself, which will likely be in some bayou town in Louisiana. Mike graciously offers to let me continue with him in the truck. I like Mike, but thirty-four hours trapped somewhere in the Pelican State getting an oil change and installing a new hose isn't exactly my idea of a weekend. I need to find a major city with an airport.

Nashville is up ahead. I get on my phone and start searching for direct flights. Bingo. There's one in a few hours. Mike and I agree that Nashville makes the most sense. He'll drop me off at a TA truck stop off I-24 not far from the airport where I can shower and change. Then I'll grab an Uber to the airport and catch my flight. There isn't a lot of time for a long goodbye. Time and money. I grab my bag as we pull into the stop, shake Mike's hand, and wish him well.

During the Uber ride to the airport, I'm struck by a chilling thought, and a quick internet search confirms my suspicion: I just showered at the same downtown Nashville truck stop where Bruce Mendenhall murdered Sarah Hulbert.

Timing is indeed everything. Twelve minutes after dropping me off at the TA, Mike texts me to say that the Gorilla Tape lost its grip. The hose burst again, and Mike pulled off the road.

CHAPTER 20

SURVIVOR TO THRIVER

Hannah decided to give sobriety one more try. If her efforts failed, she planned to end her life. She'd thought a lot about her decision; she was at peace with it.

Hannah's probation had been revoked two years after her release. She was sent back to prison for using heroin and turning tricks. Hannah believed it was that revocation that saved her life.

She was no longer eligible for the prison drug program, but Hannah was given work release. That was a big deal for someone who didn't have a dime to her name. Hannah signed up for two outside jobs. She saved her earnings while she contemplated her past, her present, and what she wanted her future to be.

In prison, as Hannah broke free from the vise grip of drugs, she experienced moments of increasing clarity. She realized she'd lost every one of her relationships. Hannah felt ashamed of her entire life. The darkness that dwelled inside convinced her she was a lost cause. She believed everyone would be better off without her.

There was a lot of praying and a lot of journaling. Hannah joined the prison therapy group. She poured herself into her work-release jobs. If she failed, it wouldn't be for lack of trying.

About six months in, there was a prison presentation by a woman from a place called Course Change. There was free food, which helped draw a crowd. This was the first time Hannah heard of a center devoted to trafficking victims. Drug recovery places, sure, but now Hannah realized there was help for people like her, people who had been dragged into the sex trade.

Until prison, Hannah had no idea of the number of inmates who had been trafficked or sold for sex. Hannah estimated it was at least 75 percent of the inmates she encountered.

For six months prior to Hannah's release, she wrote back and forth with the lady from Course Change. The woman sent Hannah an intake form and told her, "When you get out, call me." That's what Hannah did. It was her first call.

The prison work-release program required inmates to pay $700 a month for the privilege of working outside the walls. That left Hannah with $1,800. This time, there was no sober-living residence to go to, no state-subsidized funding. Hannah needed a place to stay, and she needed a way to get to and from her new job. She decided to kill two birds with one stone. Hannah took $1,200 and bought a used car—to drive and to live in.

There were long commutes from her heavy-machinery job to her regular therapy appointments at Course Change. Hannah showed up for therapy filthy, but she showed up. One of Course Change's cofounders asked Hannah where she was staying. Hannah was embarrassed to admit it, but she told her that she was homeless. When Course Change administrators offered to pay the deposit and one month's rent on an unfurnished apartment, Hannah accepted. She slept on the floor at first.

Then Course Change won a grant that allowed Hannah to

work for them. Hannah quit her job and never looked back. I asked Hannah if there was anything remarkable about that moment when everything clicked after so many excruciating attempts to drive off her demons.

"It came down to this inner desire. I never gave myself a fair shot. I always got caught up in unhealthy relationships and other distractions from what I really needed to do. I needed to do this, to cut all the crap. It was time."

I was surprised by the apparently sudden onset of what Hannah called her inner desire, her decision to cut all the crap after reaching rock bottom. But as I came to understand, there was nothing sudden about it. For Hannah, as with many addicts and trafficking victims, the downward spiral of repeated attempts at sobriety followed by multiple relapses, destruction of relationships, loss of employment, alienation from family, and run-ins with law enforcement is all part of the agonizing prequel before recovery happens. As Professors Williamson and Sepowitz explained, their programs let victims know that someone they can trust is ready to help and will be there when the victim is ready.

It's been seven years now for Hannah. Seven years sober. Therapy and life revealed what works and what doesn't work for her. This is what works for her. For now.

Hannah was promoted to a new role at Course Change, a position, funded by a grant, for a person who had Hannah's life and work experiences, the type of experiences that Hannah has shared with so many trafficking victims and, now, with me. Someday, Hannah might share her whole story with everyone, all the remarkable details. I saved the best and the worst parts for her to tell.

I asked Hannah about her approach to her work at Course Change and what she tells the women who so badly want to turn their lives around.

"I build trust. I tell them about my background—that opens the relationship. I start slowly. It's overwhelming if you tell them the whole reality, that every part of their life must be reconstructed. So I just tell them, 'I will walk hand in hand with you until you can walk on your own.' I share parts of my story when I was at my lowest, otherwise they would never guess that about me. I'm very careful not to overwhelm them, otherwise it could drive them to use drugs again. I would have to use if I considered all the work that was ahead of me! I tell them it's day by day. We are the same people."

Nancy Yarbrough spent what seemed like an eternity pondering her fate. She wasn't sure she would ever make it to what she called "the other side." She knew one thing: She was trapped in a hellish existence that she saw no way out of. Wherever she turned, Nancy remained lost in a maze of bad options.

Nancy likes to say that she made it through by God's grace. She tells everyone that *through* is her word now. "I always tell people the most powerful word that I had, that God has given me thus far, is the ability to say *through*. Because of the forward motion—I went through it, you know. I'm not in it."

Just like with Hannah, somebody was there for Nancy when she was finally ready. It is said that God meets you where you are. Since Nancy eked out her excruciating existence at truck stops, God met her in a truck.

"I got in the truck—and I always call it my olive branches

of love, my bread crumbs from God, because it was amazing things that ended up happening that kept me safe and secure. Anyway, I got in the guy's truck. He was like, 'What are you doing out here? You're not supposed to be out here. Why don't you just go to sleep.' Now, mind you, he could have been a serial killer. I wouldn't have known."

This trucker paid Nancy the cash she was supposed to hand over to her pimp. All he wanted in return was for Nancy to sleep. Once she got some shut-eye, the trucker dropped her back at her motel. That was kindness from a stranger that Nancy will never forget. But there was an entirely different experience back at the motel with someone she was all too familiar with.

Nancy turned over the night's earnings to her trafficker, a guy she thought she loved. She explained the amount was so low because a trucker had just let her fall asleep. That's when her man let her know her true value.

"And then, *pow,* he hit me. And that is when my whole world about this so-called loving, caring relationship kind of thing—it didn't make sense to me anymore."

Nancy was a lifelong people pleaser, and this violence from her man wasn't enough for her to stop trying to please him. But Nancy stored that moment away along with the words of the kind trucker who had told her that she wasn't supposed to be out there hustling.

Soon enough, there was another sign from a most unexpected messenger. Nancy had finished the night at another truck stop and was chatting with the woman who had trained her in the trade.

"She was like, 'You don't belong here. Like, you need to go home.'"

Nancy thought maybe this was a prank. Was she about to be disciplined by her man? Nancy continued talking with the woman and eventually allowed her to take her back home. Escape wasn't easy; it never is. Nancy's trafficker-boyfriend found her, intimidated her, then tried to play lovey-dovey, but Nancy wasn't having it.

The transition out of a pimp-controlled life wasn't pretty. Like Hannah, Nancy turned to self-trafficking to maintain her drug addiction. Then, also like Hannah, Nancy oversaw other women and trafficked them. It wasn't until she was thirty that Nancy was ready to go back to the lessons her preacher-father had instilled. She turned to a heavenly father, the proverbial higher power in Twelve-Step programs, for help to put an end to her drug and alcohol use. She was ready.

Trafficking victims were ready for Nancy. They needed her help. Nancy is the founder and executive director of Fresh Start Learning in Milwaukee. Fresh Start supports and advocates for victims of domestic violence and human trafficking. It's the same line of work that Hannah pursued. Or maybe the work has pursued Hannah and Nancy.

When it comes to being addicted and trafficked, Nancy's been there, done that. As she would say, she's not in it anymore, she's through it. She's not just a survivor, she's a thriver, and if she has anything to say about it, many more survivors and thrivers will find their way through it too.

EPILOGUE

Killer truckers remain a clear and present danger. It's a threat that sometimes veers far off the highway and much too close to home. In March 2023, Texas-based long-haul driver Ramin Khodakaramrezaei, thirty-eight, murdered a podcast host he was obsessed with. The trucker began stalking Zohreh Sadeghi, thirty-three, who went to court and got a temporary restraining order against him. But before police could find him to serve the order, Khodakaramrezaei found his target. He appeared at Sadeghi's suburban Seattle home and shot and killed her, her husband, and then himself.

While truckers keep killing, the FBI keeps helping police solve cold-case murders by truckers. In January 2023, James William Grimsley, a fifty-five-year-old long-hauler living in Utah, was finally arrested for allegedly murdering Terrie Ladwig, a twenty-eight-year-old trans woman, in her Concord, California, apartment. She had been beaten, strangled with a cord, and murdered almost three decades earlier, in 1994. California police said forensic evidence directed them to Grimsley.

This book started as an interest in the FBI's Highway Serial Killings Initiative but quickly became a quest to understand the cultures beneath the killings. The truckers and the trafficked, the professors and the pimps, the cops and the crime analysts took me on a journey to places I hadn't anticipated, populated by people I never knew. They allowed me into their worlds, their realities, and their stories. I learned much from each of them— enough to offer some thoughts on tackling the tough issues around trafficking victims, the people who kill them, and what the future might hold.

Our country has made inroads against the scourge of sex trafficking. Yet it's hard to counter what we can't even quantify. The estimates of the number of women, men, and children forced into sexual servitude in the United States every year vary broadly because there's no single method of capturing the data. As detailed by DeliverFund, a nonprofit intelligence group that helps train and equip police to counter human trafficking, "one study from the Department of Health and Human Services estimates the number between 240,000 and 325,000, while a report from the University of Pennsylvania says there are between 100,000 and 300,000 victims annually." We must get better at data collection if we're going to make a dent in trafficking prevention. To do that, more people need to give a damn.

Victims of sex trafficking are still among the most vulnerable people in our society. Yes, there is far less sex trade at truck stops these days, but don't be deceived. The trafficking still happens in nearby motels and massage parlors and, most of all, via the internet, the greatest force multiplier of trafficking in history.

Hannah, herself an early adopter of online ads, confirmed the shift away from truck stops and toward a more tech-driven approach to trafficking.

"There's a lot more signage today at truck stops warning about trafficking. A lot of truck stops are renovated—they don't want to return to the days of sleaze and drug sales. In my city, there are signs that warn of prosecution. The trade has shifted online: 'Let's meet at a motel' or 'Park your truck at the Walmart.' The problem hasn't gone away, it's just moved. There's also cash apps like Venmo and PayPal that make it easier for everyone—pimps, their girls, their clients—to move money around."

The shift is not unlike the transition from Dale's old-fashioned trucking to Mike's high-tech logs and trackers.

Sex ads on Craigslist are largely eliminated since that platform shut down its personal-ads sections several years ago. The notorious Backpage.com is shuttered. But there are hundreds of more sites now, more decentralized, harder to isolate and neutralize. For law enforcement, anti-trafficking groups, and legislators, it's a game of cyber-world Whac-A-Mole—take a site down, two more sites pop up. Yet the battle must continue, with increased policing of the internet and enhanced civil and criminal penalties for people and platforms that host sites where victims are trafficked.

Polaris, the anti-trafficking organization, has assembled the most comprehensive North American trafficking database. In 2018, they released results of multiyear research that found almost a thousand sex-trafficking victims were recruited online—through Facebook, dating sites, Instagram, and in chat rooms and other electronic venues, often through a technique that Polaris calls boyfriending.

Online groomers use coded language or sometimes no language at all; emojis are part of a subtle recruitment of victims. McKenzie Zahradnik, a prevention educator at ASTOP (Assist

Survivors. Treatment. Outreach. Prevention), had this revelation from her observance of online grooming: "The things that they were communicating wasn't through actual words," she said. "It was through different emojis and they meant different things. So if we take our child's phone and we're trying to look through it, do we always know what that fully means?"

Of course, internet advertisements, online recruiting schemes, and the physical presence of victims for sale at truck stops are merely public manifestations of deeper ills. As I learned from the experts, drug abuse and mental-health issues are inextricably linked to the supply side of sex trafficking. Public awareness of these problems has risen, along with a growing yet still inadequate number of treatment plans and programs.

But there's another societal aspect to trafficking that remains largely unaddressed. It's the part that few people, particularly those in power, seem willing to confront: the insatiable demand—almost entirely from men—for accessible, affordable commercial sex.

It's not that no one is working on the client, or john, side of the equation; it's just that the effort hasn't taken hold. Clearly, some of the law enforcement/social work partnerships, like the ones bolstered by Dr. Sepowitz, target the men who respond to trafficking ads. But many similar efforts, including arresting the johns, are superficial at best. There's much more work to be done.

For example, one organization created an award-winning campaign to motivate men to take a public stand against the commercial sex trade and sex trafficking. The initiative spread across the country and around the globe through the power of social media. At least 65,000 men have viewed its educational video and taken the pledge not to become part of the demand for human trafficking.

> I pledge to educate men on the importance of ending human trafficking.
>
> We pledge to work to eradicate the business of human trafficking for our women, for our men and for the world.
>
> It is my duty to not stand by and let the industry of human trafficking benefit off the back of the innocent, therefore I pledge my heart, mind, body and spirit to the eradication of an industry that seeks to destroy life rather than build it up.

Police departments, which are often male-dominated, need to take a more active role in countering trafficking. Despite all her time at truck stops, Hannah never interacted with the police there. She could count on one hand the number of times she saw what might have been an undercover officer or police vehicle even near a truck stop. I asked Dale Weaver how common it was in his time to see the police patrolling truck stops. He told me that he might have seen a police or sheriff's car once a night at a stop, but no more than that. In his years on the road—what he called his "lifetime at truck stops"—he told me the police weren't really a presence. During my week on the road with Mike in and out of truck stops, I saw the police only once—and that seemed to involve a suspicious or stolen car, not a trucker.

As for law enforcement, they would be wise to spend far less time arresting the sex-trafficked and more time identifying them as victims and sources of intelligence—about drugs, pimps, and potentially violent truckers. Hannah offered words of advice to the police about combating trafficking:

"It has to be a collective effort with the community—a holistic approach to supply and demand. It's too stovepiped. Cops do their thing; social workers do theirs. Drug treatment centers do their own thing. More partnerships are needed. There are lots of cues and signs and red flags that law enforcement misses. It's easy to turn a blind eye and not put in enough time to really have an impact."

Professors Williamson and Sepowitz would echo those sentiments. In fact, they've implemented those ideas.

In terms of impact, it's debatable whether legalizing prostitution would have any effect on actual trafficking. While legalization might free vice detectives to shift their focus away from adult sex workers who have made a choice and onto true trafficking, it might also cause law enforcement officers to throw up their hands and walk away from investigating anything related to the sex trade. Similarly, the public could be confused and assume that since prostitution was legal, all commercial sex must be legal. The empathy for victims and outcry against trafficking could be lost. And legalization wouldn't put a stop to trafficking. There will always be criminals who prey on the most vulnerable and try to make a buck on the backs of those who are unable or unwilling to break away.

Ten counties in Nevada have legalized prostitution within licensed brothels, but all is not as it seems. As Dr. Williamson explained it, many of the women in those brothels are sent there by boyfriends or pimps to earn money and send it back to them.

Right off the top, half of their earnings go to the brothel, and for some, the rest goes somewhere else. There are also strict laws requiring women to spend most of their time inside the brothel as well as restrictions that prevent the women from raising their children in Nevada. That means the workers who are mothers are kept from their kids and are largely relegated to life inside the brothel. To me, it sounds more like involuntary servitude than free enterprise.

Most important, to reduce the number of trafficked people and lessen the likelihood of more murder victims, we need more heroes like Dr. Williamson, Dr. Sepowitz, Nancy and Hannah. Individuals who devote their lives to producing not just post-trafficking survivors but lifelong thrivers.

Then there are the truckers. Young Mike doesn't need a medical or psychology degree to know what most truckers in-tuitively know—the profession is brutal on the body and brain. But most truckers might not know that there is research to back that up.

If you ask a large group of behavioral profilers, psycholo-gists, and criminologists whether serial killers are conceived in the womb or crafted during their lives, most will tell you it's a little of both—or, more likely, a lot of both. A horribly tragic mix of gene variants and misfiring brain synapses com-bined with cruel childhood home environments, neglect, and other environmental influences can produce heinous results. Of course, sometimes they don't. And sometimes, only a few of those factors are present in studies of those who kill and keep killing until they are caught.

So what is it about long-haul trucking and long-haul truckers?

Why are a significant number of truckers historically and currently associated with serial murder? Is it nature or nurture or both?

In 2020, a Canadian study led by Jennifer K. Johnson at the University of Western Ontario provided plenty of fodder for the nurture crowd. Entitled "The Health Experiences of Long-Haul Truck Drivers and Their Relationship with Their Primary Care Provider," the study found "repeated themes of isolation, dehumanization, unmet basic needs, and truckers living in a 'hidden, separate world.'"

The study was filled with accounts of systemic sleep deprivation, dangerously poor diets, lack of exercise, and the absence of regular medical care. The truckers in the study all talked about the stress of having to deliver their cargo on time, regardless of variables totally out of their control—inclement weather, unexpected traffic nightmares, border inspections, law enforcement stops, and mechanical failures.

As one trucker said, and as the Canadian study seems to confirm, "If a trucker didn't suffer from depression at the start of his career, he would by the end."

The truckers in the study were keenly aware that as they gripped the steering wheels of their rigs, they held the power of life and death. One of the study participants expressed how that felt:

"Driving a truck is not an easy job. It's a very dangerous job. It's not only like you drive; I am also trying to save everybody who is around me because those people are not aware of me, like what I can do to them."

What he can do to any of us.

That's not to say that there are any excuses or easy explanations as to why certain truckers kill. Many people experience far greater stress than long-haul truckers under similarly isolating and unhealthy circumstances for decades but never turn into serial predators. Some of them, like prisoners of war or those with horrifically abusive childhoods, go on to achieve great successes and enjoy warm relationships. One of the differences might be the distinct traits of a small subset of truckers who choose to long-haul because they are driven—perhaps subconsciously—by the opportunity for evil. For me, the question isn't so much why some truckers kill but whether we can lessen the odds of it happening.

I think we can.

First, trafficking education should be mandatory to obtain a CDL. It wouldn't take much time—perhaps no more than an hour to play an eye-opening video. Truckers in CDL classes can even be given the opportunity to take the pledge not to be part of the demand side of trafficking. It would serve as a start to men understanding that the women in those lots, in those nearby massage parlors and motels, are most likely not operating of their own free will and that the trucker's money is going straight to a pimp. It's not that such enlightenment would dissuade a killer, but it would increase trafficking awareness among a cadre of people who are more likely than others to see it, report it, and even intervene to help someone. There is at least one organization trying to accomplish this right now.

Truckers Against Trafficking (TAT) is a nonprofit organization that says it "educates, equips, and mobilizes truckers, the travel-plaza industry, and law enforcement to combat human trafficking." They take a "pro-trucking" approach that views truckers as a "positive force for good in discovering and disrupting human trafficking networks." Since its inception in 2009, TAT has trained almost a million and a half people. The organization offers a four-hour block of training to law enforcement professionals. TAT recognizes and addresses that, as positive a force as truckers might be, they also represent a portion of the demand side of the problem.

On that front, TAT offers "individuals, corporations, and men's groups" a thirty-eight-minute video called *Addressing Demand Man to Man*. Most recently TAT launched a mobile exhibit called the Freedom Drivers Project (FDP). The full-size tractor trailer, eye-catchingly wrapped, has traveled over two hundred thousand miles across forty-five states to over two hundred events, according to TAT's media platforms. The TAT website claims that "over fifty thousand truckers and others have visited the walk-through exhibit in the FDP's climate-controlled trailer." And TAT's training has paid off. Each year, the group recognizes truckers and cops who've saved lives by reporting or disrupting a trafficking situation or by aiding a victim.

Second, we should enhance health-care practices for truckers by more closely monitoring their physical and mental health and by making it harder for them to satisfy their annual checkup requirements by merely popping into a cash-only walk-in clinic for a routine once-over. All of this would take money, increase health-insurance costs, and likely reduce the supply of available truckers. The industry lobbyists would hate it, but so would the serial killers.

The mental health of truckers might also benefit from the

practice of cross-training them in more than one type of trucking, especially within companies that run a variety of truck types. Training a dry-van trucker to also haul flatbeds or reefers or tankers might help break the mind-numbing monotony they experience. More engagement with the load, more mental stimulation, could lessen the opportunity and the likelihood of killers gravitating to the job. Maybe.

Third, we should treat truckers as the essential workers that they are. Trucking is an integral part of our nation's supply chain, which means truckers are vital to our economy. In 2021, the industry earned over $875 billion in gross freight revenue. According to *Business Insider,* "grocery stores would run out of stock in three days if truckers stopped driving." Yet the country does not seem to acknowledge that truckers make all that happen.

Better pay and better working conditions; professional screening and background checks, even psychological vetting; and mandatory tracking devices regardless of independent ownership could all potentially stack the odds against serial killers or at least make it easier to catch them. Those kinds of changes would require legislation and overcoming the powerful trucking-industry lobby, and it would run into union resistance. But it's worth a try because electronic tracking also makes sense from an anti-theft perspective. Trucks are hijacked and loads get pilfered all the time. According to the FBI, cargo theft costs American shippers and truckers at least thirty billion dollars a year. A simple GPS device might catch a thief—as well as a killer.

Hannah has some insights on catching killer truckers from her own experiences. She would tell crime analysts assigned to highway murders to prioritize suspects with alcohol problems.

In Hannah's experience, those guys were the loose cannons, the most unpredictable.

"I saw some drug use by truckers, but by far, alcohol was the problem among the scariest drivers, and their real addiction was sex. Look for truckers with few or no relationships. Men with a deep sense of rejection by women, unassimilated into society, suffering from social anxiety, painfully introverted with a history of violence."

I asked Hannah who she thought was more likely to be a serial killer, the corporate trucker or the guy who owned and operated his own truck. That's when she shared the story of a friend of hers, a fellow inmate, whose regular trucker client parked at a truck stop but rented a car and a motel room. He'd use his car to take Hannah's friend to dinner, then they'd head to the motel.

"He beat and raped my friend—but his truck never entered the picture. He did this crime during his downtime."

If that trucker was corporate, then he'd figured out a way to beat the truck's tracking devices: just rent a car on your downtime. If he was independent, no one cared where he was or what he did. It didn't matter. But it mattered to Hannah's friend. When Hannah's parole was revoked and she was held in lockdown before she was transported back to prison, she spotted her friend on the jail television. Her friend had been found dead by the side of the road. Hannah doesn't think it was drugs. She's convinced someone killed her.

All of this presumes that there is some inherent uniqueness to the trucking industry and its established link to serial killing, that somehow, if the need for long-haul truckers vaporizes, we'll see a corresponding drop in the number of serial murders.

Maybe not.

Enzo Yaksic, a founder of the Atypical Homicide Research Group at Northeastern University in Boston, said that serial killers characteristically take "unremarkable jobs, mostly in blue-collar fields, and figure out ways to use them in their favor." Yaksic explained, "Those that punch a clock can fade into the background. And performing routine tasks that don't require excessive concentration helps them save mental energy. Their emotional intelligence is reserved for learning how best to exploit others for their own gain rather than for the good of the company's bottom line."

In other words, if the day ever comes when there is no need for long-haul truckers or there are far fewer truckers, those individuals who are predisposed to killing will simply find another way to keep on killing.

So where will the killers go next? Most likely, they'll make the same transition that their victims and other kinds of murderers have made—they'll move right on to the internet. Undoubtedly, some long-haul killers are already there. It makes perfect sense. Researchers D. J. Williams, Jeremy Thomas, and Michael Arntfield in a 2017 article for *Leisure Sciences* wrote about it.

"The disappearance of once traditional career paths will obviously have profound effects not only on the jobs held by offenders but also how they acquire their victims. Serial killers once used the guise of their employment to stalk and acquire specific victims or types of victims. But new research suggests that leisure activities . . . including online interactions, may be the new avenue through which serial killers troll for their victims."

How long might it be before killer truckers start trading their semis for the cyber world in large enough numbers that the FBI's HSK team notices? That day is nearer than you think.

THE FUTURE IS NOW AS DRIVERLESS TRUCKING HITS NATION'S HIGHWAYS
Markie Martin, Tom Palmer
April 22, 2022

(NewsNation)—Many Americans might not realize that driverless tractor-trailers are currently navigating the nation's highways, hitting the open road with absolutely nobody behind the wheel. . . .

Autonomous driving technology company TuSimple was founded in San Diego in 2015 with a mission to improve the safety and efficiency of the trucking industry.

TuSimple is a developer of heavy-duty, self-driving trucks and the autonomous startup has already created a freight network along the Sun Belt from Phoenix to Houston.

"This is better, no doubt about it," said Jim Mullen, chief administrator and legal officer for TuSimple. . . .

"It doesn't get mad, there's no road rage, it's in no hurry," Mullen said. "It doesn't have the characteristics that we as humans sometimes have."

ACKNOWLEDGMENTS

This was not an easy book to write. The subject matter—serial-killer truckers, their victims, sex trafficking, and the professionals who strive to stop the killings, reduce trafficking, and aid victims—isn't pleasant. Yet it's a story that needed to be told, if only to shed light on places left in the dark for too long.

My task was made easier by the kind people who graciously offered their time and shared their passions with me. I would not have wanted to attempt this project without the expertise of Dr. Celia Williamson of the University of Toledo and Dr. Dominique Roe-Sepowitz of Arizona State University. The work they do in support of sex-trafficking victims brings hope to those who most need it. That's why I've provided their organizations with financial donations. If you feel similarly inclined, please consider donating to Starfish Place via the Venmo application at @starfish-fundaz or at phoenix.gov/housing/findingaffordable rental/starfish-place, and to RISE at rise@use.salvationarmy.org.

My journey into the world of long-haul trucking was illuminated by Dale, the Spirit of Trucking Past, and Mike, the Spirit of Trucking Present. If all young long-haul drivers are like Mike, our roads and our cargo are safer and more secure than I originally imagined. Only a tiny fraction of truckers are responsible for the murders in the FBI's Highway Serial Killings Initiative. Truckers are a crucial component of our nation's supply chain.

They are essential workers who don't deserve to be tarnished by those who dishonor the profession.

Crime analyst Terri Turner of the Oklahoma State Bureau of Investigation retired soon after our discussions. I'm happy for her, yet I know that crime fighting across her state is diminished without her decades of experience. I'm grateful that the woman who first recognized that the murders happening across state lines were linked and that they required a national approach was able to speak with me.

FBI crime analyst Catherine DeVane didn't know it, but she planted the seed for this book during an FBI-approved conversation about violent crime analysis. When I told my literary agent, Peter McGuigan of Ultra Literary, about my talk with Catherine, he exclaimed, "That's your next book!" I guess he was right.

Victims are the heart of this book. Their stories and their willingness to share them bring a glimmer of hope to anyone who has hit rock bottom. Women like Hannah and Nancy have not only survived addiction and trafficking but thrived in its aftermath. Their decision to dedicate their lives to helping others who face the monumental challenge of climbing out of hell reflects their resolve to turn victimhood into victory.

At Mariner/HarperCollins, vice president and publisher Peter Hubbard helped make this book better than it would have been without him. Assistant editor Jessica Vestuto was gracious and patient with me, and copyeditor Tracy Roe polished my manuscript with precision.

While delving into the pure evil embedded in the horror stories of serial killings, I never lost sight of the fact that I was surrounded by the light and love of my wife and family. They were the antidote to the darkness.

As required of books written by former FBI employees, this manuscript underwent a prepublication review to identify any potential disclosures of classified or sensitive information, but it was not reviewed by the Bureau for editorial content or accuracy. The FBI does not endorse or validate any information described in this book. The opinions expressed are mine and not those of the FBI or any other federal government agency or department. The factual descriptions of FBI investigations I did not directly work on are based primarily on public news reports, interviews, and other source reporting, not on information I learned while serving as an FBI special agent.

INTRODUCTION

PAGE

1   *It was early morning:* Brian Myers, "Inside Robert Ben Rhoades' Traveling Torture Chamber," *Grunge,* November 24, 2022, https://www.grunge.com/1116029/inside-robert-ben-rhoades-traveling-torture-chamber/.

1   *final murder victim:* Vanessa Veselka, "The Truck Stop Killer," *GQ,* October 24, 2012.

3   *FBI agent Mark Young:* Marco Margaritoff, "The Chilling Story of Regina Kay Walters," *All That's Interesting,* February 22, 2022, https://allthatsinteresting.com/regina-kay-walters.

2. THE FBI CRIME ANALYST

19   *Nashville Metro PD homicide detective Pat Postiglione:* Brad Hunter, "*Monster City*: New Tome on World's Greatest Cold Case Detective," *Toronto Sun,* October 14, 2018.

19   *Illinois-based Bruce D. Mendenhall:* "Man Charged in Truck Stop Slaying; Suspected in at Least 5 Others," Associated Press, July 13, 2007, https://www.actionnews5.com/story/6783305/man-charged-in-truck-stop-slaying-suspected-in-at-least-5-others/.

23   *It took just three days:* Ashe Schow, "Trucker Who Admitted to Killing NYC Model Gets Sentenced," *Daily Wire,* November 8, 2022, https://www.dailywire.com/news/trucker-who-admitted-to-killing-nyc-model-gets-sentenced.

26   *Linda Schacke was able:* John North and Leslie Ackerson, "Appalachian Unsolved: The Trucker Who Liked Redheads," WBIR.com, June 3, 2020, https://www.wbir.com/article/news/investigations

/appalachian-unsolved/appalachian-unsolved-the-trucker-intrigued
-by-serial-killers/51-624ef38c-0372-42a4-8bee-25b2b1647c95.

28 *"I always slept well at night"*: Alberto Luperson, "Serial Killer's Chilling and Cheerful Confession on Podcast Leads to Search for Possible Location of Victim," Lawandcrime.com, September 4, 2020, https://lawandcrime.com/crazy/serial-killers-chilling-and-cheerful-confession-on-podcast-leads-to-search-for-possible-location-of-victim/.

3. GIRLS NEXT DOOR

34 *TEDx talk:* Nancy Yarbrough, "Myths, Misconceptions, Mysteries and Mistakes of the Sex Trade," TEDx talk, February 13, 2018, https://nancy-theexodus.com/about-us/.

35 *"So, my journey began"*: Mike Woods, "I Went Through It: Wisconsin Woman Who Was Trafficked Helps Other Victims," Spectrum News1.com, April 28, 2023, https://spectrumnews1.com/wi/milwaukee/news/2023/04/18/part-5--wisconsin-woman-who-was-human-trafficked-helps-other-victims.

35 *"They took advantage"*: Yarbrough, "Myths, Misconceptions."

35 *"bullied, ostracized"*: Woods, "I Went Through It."

37 *"That caused me to be raped"*: Woods, "I Went Through It."

37 *"I'm crying out"*: Yarbrough, "Myths, Misconceptions."

39 *"fear, vulnerability"*: Yarbrough, "Myths, Misconceptions."

39 *nothing traumatic ever happened:* Yarbrough, "Myths, Misconceptions."

41 *drug was cocaine:* Yarbrough, "Myths, Misconceptions."

43 *Garry Dean Artman:* Gina Tron, "Garry Dean Artman Arrested for 1996 Murder of Sharon Hammack," Oxygen.com, August 22, 2022, https://www.oxygen.com/crime-news/garry-dean-artman-arrested-1996-murder-sharon-hammack.

4. THE PIONEER PROFESSOR

50 *part of their study:* Celia Williamson and Lynda M. Baker, "Women in Street-Based Prostitution: A Typology of Their Work Styles," *Journal of Qualitative Social Work* 8, no. 1 (March 2009).

5. OLD-TIMER

69 New York Times *called them:* Martin Waldron, "U.S. Crackdown on Amphetamines Driving Up Prices," *New York Times*, January 22, 1972.

6. MONDAY WITH MIKE

85 *the best truck-friendly Walmarts:* truckerpath.com, https://truckerpath.com/trucker-path-app/walmart-with-truck-parking/.

7. THE OKLAHOMA CRIME ANALYST

102 *That's what former McIntosh:* Bob Doucette, "A Hint of the Sinister," *Oklahoman,* April 23, 2001.

8. CROSSING THE RUBICON

107 *"He was way older than me":* Woods, "I Went Through It."
108 *"started experiencing a different type":* Woods, "I Went Through It."
108 *no baby steps:* Woods, "I Went Through It."
108 *"We had to be groomed":* Woods, "I Went Through It."
109 *"We got paid more":* Woods, "I Went Through It."
109 *"It just depends on the day":* Woods, "I Went Through It."
109 *once she was trafficked:* Woods, "I Went Through It."
111 *"Every trafficking situation is unique":* "Myths, Facts and Statistics," Polaris Project, https://polarisproject.org/myths-facts-and-statistics/.
113 *A 2020 study:* Christopher M. Jones, Rita K. Noonan, and Wilson M. Compton, "Prevalence and Correlates of Ever Having a Substance Use Problem and Substance Use Recovery Status Among Adults in the United States, 2018," *Drug and Alcohol Dependence* 214 (September 2020), https://doi.org/10.1016/j.drugalcdep.2020.108169.
113 *victory took almost a decade:* Brian Mann, "There Is Life After Addiction. Most People Recover," NPR.org, January 15, 2022, https://www.npr.org/2022/01/15/1071282194/addiction-substance-recovery-treatment.

10. TUESDAY WITH MIKE

129 *"But not Vafeades"*: Eric Peterson, "The Case of the Vampire Trucker," Vice.com, July 7, 2016, https://www.vice.com/en/article /9b8wav/the-case-of-the-vampire-trucker.

11. THE OKLAHOMA CRIME ANALYST

136 *"I just broke your neck"*: "Suspect Arrested for Rape and Attempted Murder," ActionNews5.com, September 22, 2004, https://www .actionnews5.com/story/2333343/suspect-arrested-for-rape-and -attempted-murder-now-at-center-of-serial-killer-investigation/.

136 *"He's probably the biggest teddy bear"*: Jim Pressman, "Family of Lincoln Truck Driver Accused of Assault, Rape, Speaks Out," KLKN-TV, September 20, 2004, https://www.klkntv.com/family -of-lincoln-truck-driver-accused-of-assault-rape-speaks-out/.

139 *"She was a sweet girl"*: Amber Advocate, 2016 Tribal Symposium, https://www.amberadvocate.org/amber-feature/she-was-a-sweet -girl-and-did-not-deserve-to-die/.

139 *An FBI agent who testified:* Michael Baker, "Federal Judge Calls Pimp Heartless," *Oklahoman,* March 5, 2005.

140 *"My nephew made a comment"*: "John Robert Williams," Murder pedia.org, https://murderpedia.org/male.W/w/williams-john-robert.htm.

142 *"The second she tapped on my window"*: Scott Glover, "FBI Makes a Connection Between Long-Haul Truckers, Serial Killings," *Los Angeles Times,* April 5, 2009.

142 *Which is precisely what John Williams did:* Glover, "FBI Makes a Connection."

13. A STARFISH IN THE DESERT

150 *In one version:* "The Tale of the Starfish," thestarfishchange.org, https://www.thestarfishchange.org/starfish-tale.

154 *the DOJ seized Backpage.com:* Press release, "U.S. Department of Justice Seizes Backpage.com," U.S. Department of Justice, April 9, 2018, https://www.justice.gov/opa/pr/justice-department-leads-effort -seize-backpagecom-internet-s-leading-forum-prostitution-ads.

14. WEDNESDAY WITH MIKE

170 *over ten billion dollars a year:* "Travel Centers of America, Inc. Announces First Quarter 2023 Financial Results," Business wire.com, April 26, 2023, https://www.businesswire.com/news /home/20230426005864/en/TravelCenters-of-America-Inc. -Announces-First-Quarter-2023-Financial-Results.

15. THE OKLAHOMA CRIME ANALYST

177 *FBI PRESS RELEASE:* Federal Bureau of Investigation, April 7, 2021, https://www.fbi.gov/contact-us/field-offices/memphis/news /press-releases/fbi-seeking-potential-victims-in-brian-t-summerson -and-pierre-l-washington-investigation.

16. THURSDAY WITH MIKE

182 *CBs were ubiquitous:* "CB Radios: The Original Social Media for Truckers on the Road," gokoho.com, https://www.gokoho.com /blog/cb-radios-and-trucker-handles.

19. SATURDAY WITH MIKE

224 *The sheriff claimed:* Isaac Calvert, "Horse Cave Adult Bookstore Closes After Illegal Activity, Two Deaths Reported," WBKO/Gray News, September 7, 2022, https://www.wbko.com/2022/09/08 /new-details-horse-cave-adult-book-store-closes-after-illegal -activity-two-deaths-reported/.

20. SURVIVOR TO THRIVER

230 *Nancy likes to say:* Woods, "I Went Through It."
230 *"I got in the truck":* Woods, "I Went Through It."
231 *"And then,* pow, *he hit me":* Woods, "I Went Through It."
232 *"She was like":* Woods, "I Went Through It."

EPILOGUE

233 *long-haul driver Ramin Khodakaramrezaei:* Vanessa Bein, "Podcaster and Her Husband Allegedly Murdered by Obsessive Stalker," Lawandcrime.com, March 12, 2023, https://lawandcrime.com/crime/podcaster-and-her-husband-allegedly-murdered-by-obsessive-stalker/.

235 *Polaris calls boyfriending:* "Looking for Love Online This Valentine's Day?," Polaris Project, February 7, 2019, https:polarisproject.org/blog/2019/02/looking-for-love-online-this-valentines-day/.

235 *McKenzie Zahradnik:* Mike Woods, "How Sex Trafficking Victims Are Lured In," SpectrumNews1.com, April 25, 2023, https://spectrumnews1.com/wi/milwaukee/news/2023/04/19/part-2--how-sex-trafficking-victims-are-lured-in.

246 *THE FUTURE IS NOW:* Markie Martin and Tom Palmer, "The Future Is Now as Driverless Trucking Hits Nation's Highways," NewsNation, April 22, 2022, https://www.newsnationnow.com/us-news/truck-week/future-driverless-trucking-highways/.